AROUND THE DELAWARE ARC

101 PEOPLE, PLACES, AND LORE

EDWARD SEARL

THE ROYAL NONESUCH PRESS

ISBN-13: 978-0615830230
ISBN-10: 0615830234
LCCN: 2013910555

Front cover: Gilpin House and Lafayette Sycamore at Brandywine Battlefield State Park
Back cover: Spring House at Brandywine Battlefield State Park

THE ROYAL NONESUCH PRESS
WILMINGTON, DE

CONTENTS

Contents

Contents

Contents

Contents

We did it together.

Thank you, Ellie

INTRODUCTION

A LANDSCAPE OF MEANING

SOUTHEASTERN PENNSYLVANIA (CHESTER AND DELAWARE Counties) and Northern Delaware (New Castle County) is a unique geography, a compact area traversed by an unusual arc boundary that extends from the Delaware River in the east to the Mason Dixon Line in the west.

Great ages of Nature reaching back a half billion years shaped this Space. Around the Delaware Arc, a relatively recent veneer of human habitation has deposited layers of meaning.

This accessible Space is part of the Appalachian Piedmont as it reaches toward a coastal plain south of Wilmington, Delaware. The beguiling landscape of time-sculptured hills and valleys features a number of creeks that once powered early American mills, including the Brandywine Creek that lends its name to much of the region's lore. From 1790 through 1840, this was America's breadbasket, rich farmland cultivated by industrious farmers, many of German origin, who came to this land because of the religious toleration afforded by William Penn.

Penn's famous grant (1681) allowed him to implement a vision of a Quaker colony that not only ensured religious freedom to his own persecuted sect, The Religious Society of Friends, but also to all other Christians of good faith. Penn's "Holy Experiment," only partially realized in Penn's era, endures. A Quaker sensibility lingers.

A profound influence on the region is the du Pont family, who came to America from France as political exiles in 1800 and used the waterpower of the Brandywine to make black powder. The dynastic family profited greatly from a recession-proof industry fueled by a succession of wars, while contributing to western expansion. At the end of the nineteenth century, the wealthiest of the du Pont family began to transform great tracts of Brandywine Valley land into country manor estates. As a consequence, much of the region did not experience twentieth century suburban development and remains "green."

Today, several decades of concerted preservation, conservation, and a little remediation recommend that Delaware be granted its first national park, anchored by a Brandywine Valley tract of land known as the Woodlawn Trust, an early twentieth century legacy of William Poole Bancroft who made his turn-of the century fortune from a famous Wilmington textile mill.

The region Around the Delaware Arc (a 22.57-mile compound circle with a 12-mile radius) is truly remarkable for its extensive green space affording many opportunities for natural recreation and for a concentration of historical places to explore and experience.

There is a Brandywine Mythos still evolving that brings together the landscape and the peoples who have inhabited the landscape: a Humanistic Geography of Space defined by a host of varied Places and their emotional connections with passing visitors, and even more so for residents.

These 101 brief narratives illuminate some of those Places with additional persons and lore chosen from a ten-mile swath on either side of the Delaware Arc. Many of the chosen Places, persons, and lore are familiar. But a reader will find a number of lesser known, if known at all, worthy additions to the natural and cultural geography of Southeastern Pennsylvania and Northern Delaware—surely enchanted Space.

This collection is an introduction for visitors seeking to get acquainted with and a deepening for locals regarding a Landscape of Meaning. It is also a call for a Delaware National Park to protect and promote that meaning.

Loosely organized, this collection is not intended to be read from cover to cover. It is a reference work of varied places, organized by areas and themes to inform and delight the reader. It encourages the reader to experience and emotionally interact with those places.

Enjoy. Explore. Discover.
Enter a Landscape of Meaning.

PRELUDE

AN ANCIENT GEOLOGY

THE SCULPTED LANDSCAPE PLUS THE prominent rocks Around the Delaware Arc give mute witness to dramatic geological events that began more than 500 million years ago.

What is now known as the Wilmington Complex originated from an arc of ancient oceanic volcanos. Over eons, the volcanos drifted onto the continental crust. As a result of the collision, continental rock, volcanic rock, sedimentary rock, and strata of sediment from the ocean floor were folded, sheared, and buried some 11 to 13 miles deep. Under extreme pressure and heat reaching 1600 degrees Fahrenheit, these strata melted and metamorphosed. Subsequent tectonic activity uplifted these deeply buried, transformed rocks to create the Appalachian Mountains. This great mountain range stood in the midst of one supercontinent (Pangea), formed about 300 million years ago.

Some 225 million years ago, continents began to drift apart, giving shape to North America. Eons of monumental uplift, erosion, and deposit shaped the Appalachian foothills—the Piedmont.

To a knowledgeable observer, the region Around the Delaware Arc, the time-shaped contours of the eastern reach of the Appalachian Piedmont, insinuates ancient, almost incomprehensible geological epochs of stupendous mountain building processes, followed by an evolution of erosion, sedimentation, and uplift that began more than 300 million years. Rocks, one of the region's prominent features, reveal a great geologic story, a drama unlike any other. For instance, a mass of granite in Arden, Delaware, radiometrically dates to being 500 million years old.

Rocks, especially the massive deposits of granite along the Brandywine Creek, as well as a panoply of surface boulders large and small throughout the Piedmont, testify to a cataclysmic geologic epic fashioned by time into the soothing landscape of Southeastern Pennsylvania and Northern Delaware that exists today.

CURIOUS BOUNDARIES

1 - The Delaware Arc

IN 1681, CHARLES II SETTLED a family debt owed to William Penn's father by granting William a parcel of land west of the Delaware River between the fortieth and forty-third parallels. The grant had one exclusion: the land within a 12-mile circle around New Castle (now Delaware), which James, the Duke of York and Charles II's brother, had already claimed as his own.

In 1682, Charles II formally granted to James land within a 12-mile circle around New Castle on the Delaware River. James, who had vast holdings from New England to New Jersey, held a sort of squatter's sovereignty over the region west of the Delaware River. He had already divided his holdings along the Delaware River into three counties, known as the Three Lower Counties.

Later in 1682, upon Penn's petition, James deeded to Penn the Three Lower Counties. Penn wanted to ensure ocean access to his colony. (Philadelphia was too far up the Delaware River to be secure from blockade.) James apparently had significant regard for the Penn family, particularly Penn's father Admiral William Penn, and gave his son control over the additional land.

Though under Penn's control after 1682, the identity of the Three Lower Counties remained distinct from Pennsylvania. The Three Lower Counties established its own assembly in 1704. In July 1776, Delaware became an independent state, composed of these three counties.

Beginning in 1701, a succession of surveys measured the Delaware Arc from several sites in New Castle with varying success that resulted in the famous Wedge at its Western end where the Arc met Pennsylvania and Maryland. Throughout the nineteenth century, jurisdiction over The Wedge was ambiguous among the three states. No state exercised control and The Wedge became a place for illegal activities such as prize fights and boxing.

As a result of an 1892 survey, The Wedge became Delaware property and a sliver of land east of The Wedge known as The Horn was given to Pennsylvania. New Jersey disputed the Arc's terminus on their Delaware River Shore (rather than the customary middle of the river)

through the early years of the twentieth-first century.

As it exists today, the Delaware Arc is a 22.57-mile compound circle, comprised of a series of small arcs based on a succession of surveys. It traverses southern Delaware and Chester Counties in Pennsylvania and northern New Castle County of Delaware, a region of rolling hills and winding creeks of the Piedmont. At the center of the circumference, the Brandywine Creek falls and winds toward Wilmington.

2 - DELAWARE AND NEW JERSEY BOUNDARY

COMMONLY, A RIVER BOUNDARY TRAVELS down the middle of the river. This is not the case with the boundary between Delaware and New Jersey.

Within the famous 12-mile arc around New Castle, dating back to Penn's original land grant from Charles II in 1681, a circle of land was excluded because it was under the control of James, the Duke of York. (James would become James II.) That circle extended to the New Jersey riverbank.

When James ceded his Three Lower Counties to Penn in 1682, the circle boundary continued to have authority to the New Jersey shoreline. (It did not apply to land within New Jersey because that involved an earlier royal grant.) That very odd boundary continues through today.

Just as the western terminus of the Delaware Arc and the famous Wedge caused dispute among Pennsylvania, Maryland, and Delaware through 1921, so the eastern boundary of the Delaware Arc has caused dispute as recently as 2008.

The Supreme Court had settled an 1877 dispute over fishing rights and a 1934 dispute over oyster beds, in both instances upholding Delaware's claims to the New Jersey shore within the 12-mile circle. In 2007, the Supreme Court heard another New Jersey claims to a boundary in the middle of the Delaware River. The contention involved a proposed liquefied natural gas (LNG) terminal off the New Jersey shore, but within the 12-mile circle. Delaware once again resisted, claiming its historic boundary to the New Jersey shoreline. In 2008, the Court decided in favor of Delaware. The LNG facility was not built.

3 - THE MASON DIXON LINE

ROYAL LAND GRANTS TO THE Calverts (Maryland, 1632) and William Penn (Pennsylvania, 1681) overlapped and were therefore ambiguous. In addition, James, the Duke of York had squatter's sovereignty over an area extending into the peninsula shared with Maryland and Virginia (today's Delmarva Peninsula.) James divided the area he claimed into three counties. Penn's grant excluded a 12-mile circle of James's land centered on New Castle on the Delaware River.

The Lower Counties were soon gifted (1683) to Penn by James and annexed into the Penn holdings.

In 1683, Calvert and Penn interests began negotiations to establish a common east-west boundary between the grants. The negotiations failed. The Committee for Trade and Plantations intervened, ruling that the boundary between Maryland and the Three Lower Counties would extend north from a midpoint of the Delmarva Peninsula, to run tangent to the 12-mile arc. The Maryland Pennsylvania east-west border was to run west along a parallel (line of latitude) 15 miles south of Philadelphia's southernmost limit.

These vague boundaries resulted in a number of disputes between Maryland and Pennsylvania, including Cresap's War (1730-1738) that caused the Crown to intervene. A settlement (1732) imposed by the Crown failed to settle the boundary to either colony's satisfaction. In 1760, the Crown demanded that the Calvert interests accept what are now the boundaries of Delaware, Maryland, and Pennsylvania.

Enter the British surveyors Charles Mason and Jeremiah Dixon. They were engaged in

1763 by the proprietors of Maryland and Pennsylvania to come into accord with the Court of Chancery's rulings.

Mason and Dixon were gifted surveyors who used state of the art instruments. From 1764 through 1767 they successfully established the boundaries between the two colonies, with one exception, a "wedge" shaped parcel where the Lower Colonies (Delaware), Pennsylvania, and Maryland met. Delaware claimed The Wedge, while the Mason Dixon survey gave it to Pennsylvania, which made no sense since it was below the proposed 40th line of latitude.

Jurisdiction over The Wedge was not finally settled until 1921.

In the political agitation preceding the Civil War, the Mason Dixon Line came to represent the geographic division between the Slave and the Free States–the South and the North.

To an informed eye, it remembers original land grants by the British Crown made to the Calverts and Penns, plus the convergent interests of James, the Duke of York, represented by the 12-mile arc, and of course, the skill and thoroughness of two dedicated surveyors.

The surveyors used the John Harlan House, Route 162 and Star Gazer Road, as their base.

4 - THE WEDGE

THE NORTHWEST CORNER OF DELAWARE, where the Delaware Arc meets the Mason Dixon Line (between Pennsylvania and Maryland) is a wedge shaped parcel of land: 3.574 miles along its north-south side, 0.789 mile across at the top, and completed by a 3.674-mile segment of the Circle. After being granted statehood in 1776, Delaware claimed some 800 acres of The Wedge. (The Wedge was also known as The Flatiron and The Thorn.)

Throughout the nineteenth century, both Pennsylvania and Delaware claimed this small plot, though Pennsylvania's claim was tenuous, since its southern border could not extend below Maryland's northern border. At one time, Pennsylvania offered to grant The Wedge to Delaware; Delaware refused the offer, contending it was not Pennsylvania's property to give.

Jurisdiction over The Wedge resulted in a sort of "no man's land" with none of the three states policing it. Reputedly, throughout the nineteenth century, it was a place for illegal activities: gambling, prize and cockfights, duels, and hiding-out from the law.

A U. S. Coast and Geodetic Survey measured the area in 1892-93 and placed a definitive boundary marker at the "top of The Wedge Line." Delaware finally accepted this survey in 1921, ending the long dispute and decades of ambiguity.

Delaware State Routes 273 and 896 traverse The Wedge, passing among the three states.

5 - THE HORN

I N 1892-93 SURVEY, COMMISSIONED BY Delaware and Pennsylvania, to settle the disputed area known as The Wedge, resulted in a second piece of land being surveyed and reassigned.

From a point 2000 feet east of where the Arc met the Line at the Top of The Wedge (an extension of the original Mason Dixon Line) and continuing along the arc to just west of Centerville was a thin slice of land, known as The Horn.

The commission that granted The Wedge to Delaware granted The Horn to Pennsylvania.

Delaware did not ratify the commission's settlement until 1921, supposedly because a number of residents of The Horn did not want to become Pennsylvanians.

6 – STAR GAZER'S STONE

DECADES OF SQUABBLES AND ARMED conflict between Pennsylvania and Maryland regarding the border of their respective holdings resulted in the intervention of the Crown in 1760. Royal decree established that the border between the two interests ran directly west from the southern-most habitation of Philadelphia.

The Penns and Calverts agreed upon this line. After two surveys failed to measure the Arc accurately, they sought more skilled surveyors. The Astronomer Royal of the Royal Greenwich Observatory recommended his assistant Charles Mason. He was joined by the surveyor Jeremiah Dixon.

Mason and Dixon arrived in Philadelphia in 1763 with the best of contemporary equipment and resources: several telescopes, a reflecting quadrant, a precision clock, measuring rods and chains, logarithm and trigonometric tables, and star almanacs. They first determined that the southernmost limit of Philadelphia was the north wall of a house on Cedar Street (now 30 South Street).

They reckoned, if they carried the survey line due west, they would have had to cross the Delaware River two times, making for considerable difficulties. Instead, in January 1764, they travelled 31 miles due west to a location between the two branches of the Brandywine Creek, an open site in Embreeville, on a farm owned by John Harlan.

Here they set a boulder firmly in the ground, the starting point for their observations, measurements, and calculations. The stone at their observatory's center became known as the Star Gazer Stone. Mason and Dixon set their instruments on it. During that winter, by observing eight stars, they determined the precise latitude of that point.

They launched their famous survey in April, setting stones to mark the boundary between Pennsylvania and Maryland. During the following winter, they returned to the Harlan Farm to continue their observations, measurements, and calculations. In February 1765, they determined the longitude of the Star Gazer's Stone, making that spot the most accurately measured point in America to date.

Now under the control of the National Lands Trust (ChesLen Preserve), the Star Gazer Stone sits (unmarked), embedded in concrete within a low wall in the quiet village of Embreeville. The Harlan House, (a private residence), where Mason and Dixon wintered, is nearby.

The stone is easily accessed on Star Gazer Road, where Route 162 and Star Gazer Road intersect. At that intersection is the John Harlan House.

7 - WEST POST MARK'D

THE FAMOUS MASON AND DIXON Survey (1764-1767) settled the boundary dispute that had simmered for decades between the Penn and Calvert interests that established Pennsylvania and Maryland. When the dispute broke out into armed conflict in the 1730s, the Crown intervened and imposed a boundary. It took another thirty years before a definitive survey of that boundary was accomplished by the British team of Charles Mason and Jeremiah Dixon.

Mason and Dixon were skilled surveyor/scientists. They had state of the art equipment to reckon location by celestial measurement.

The east-west boundary's latitude was arbitrarily determined by the Crown to begin 15 miles south of Philadelphia's southernmost habitation. However, the actual boundary between the two colonies began more than 30 miles to the West, where Maryland and Pennsylvania met at the curious northern boundary of the Lower Counties known as the Delaware Arc.

Upon arrival, Mason and Dixon determined the latitude of the southernmost part of Philadelphia. They next established a sighting spot on an immovable boulder 15 miles to the south and some 31 miles due west at Embreeville, Chester County, Pennsylvania, near the West Branch of the Brandywine Creek. The exact spot is remembered as the Star Gazer Stone and can be visited today.

After a winter's calculations in Embreeville that firmly established latitude, in the early months of 1764, the surveyors moved 15 miles due south. According to Mason's journal, "The point 15 miles South of the Southernmost Point of the City of Philadelphia is situated in Mill Creek Hundred in the County of Newcastle, in a Plantation belonging to Mr. Alexander Bryan."

The survey team drove a sturdy oak post deep into the ground at that spot and painted the post white with "west" painted on the west facing side. This important marker (some would say the beginning of the Mason and Dixon Line) was known as "Post Mark'd West." Its very accurate location was 31 miles due west and 15 south of the southernmost part of Philadelphia.

Today that spot is within White Clay Creek State Park. Though the actual oak post has long been gone, in 1952, the owner of the land, S. Hallock du Pont installed a granite shaft marker.

"Post Mark'd West" can be reached by a short side trail off Bryan's Field Trail in the Possum Hill section of White Clay Creek State Park, 880 New London Road, Newark, Delaware.

8 - TICKING TOMB

IN THE GRAVEYARD OF THE London Tract Primitive Baptist Meeting House, Landenberg, Pennsylvania, a stone marks the grave of Fithian Minuit. If you place your ear on the level marker, local legend maintains, you will hear the ticking of a watch–not just any watch but the watch of Charles Mason of the famous Mason and Dixon surveyor team.

The legend builds on historical fact: Mason participated and received a cash prize in a British contest regarding a more accurate means for determining longitude–the Longitude Prize. Legend contends that Mason was working on a chronometer (a very accurate timepiece or watch) as part of the contest. Supposedly, he had a working model of such a chronometer with him as he passed through the region during the celebrated survey (circa 1765) that established the Mason and Dixon Line.

A fishmonger from the Elk River region approached the survey team with fish to sell to the party. With her was a very chubby, some say obese, baby, Fithian Minuit, who had an omnivorous appetite. He would put anything in his mouth and swallow it. Perhaps chubby Fithian was fussing while his mother was attending to business. Mason's assistant tried to calm the child by dangling the watch to distract him. Or perhaps Fithian found it on his own foraging in Mason's tent. In any event, Fithian snatched and swallowed the one-of-a-kind timepiece. All efforts to dislodge the chronometer failed. The legend continues that Mason put a benign curse on the child, involving the watch.

Fithian grew up to marry Martha. Early in their relationship, she heard his chest ticking. He told her the story. He further promised that the ticking would demonstrate his love for her throughout their life together, even to eternity.

Fittingly, Fithian became a watchmaker.

In death, the couple lay together, side-by-side in the Landenberg graveyard. When conditions are just right, by placing an ear on the marker, the ticking might be heard.

Locals further contend that Edgar Allan Poe, hearing the story, came to Fithian and Martha's graves, heard the ticking, and found inspiration for his famous story "The Tell Tale Heart."

Just beyond the gate to the graveyard is a heart shaped marker of John Devonald. Adjacent is a flat marker with the letters R.C. or R.S. This is Fithian Minuit's grave.

An extended and most charming account of "The Ticking Stone" with details of Fithian Minuit's fabled life is contained in *Tales of the Chesapeake* (1880) by George Alfred Townsend.

The London Tract Meeting House is located at 405 Sharpless Road, Landenberg, Pennsylvania.

9 - OLD NEW CASTLE COURTHOUSE

OF THE SITES THAT RELATE to the curious 12-mile Arc that separates Delaware and Pennsylvania's border, the Old New Castle Courthouse at New Castle, Delaware, is truly central.

The cupola at the building's top was one of the starting points for Mason and Dixon's celebrated survey (1764-1767) that settled a long-standing boundary dispute between the interests of the Calverts (Maryland) and the Penns (Pennsylvania). The cupola center point was firmly determined in 1750.

From that point, the surveyors established the center of the 12-mile arc that defined the boundaries where Pennsylvania, Maryland, and the Three Lower Counties that became Delaware. (Recent surveys of the Arc have used a point several thousand feet northwest of the original cupola point.)

The courthouse dates from 1732. With occasional court sessions held through today, the courthouse is the longest continuously operating court in the country.

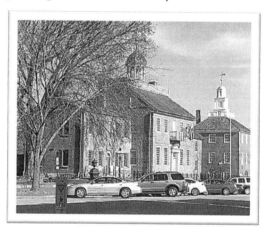

It is located in the midst of a well-maintained and celebrated historic district some five by four blocks, along the Delaware River. This historic district of 135 acres has some 460 historic buildings (1700-1940), brick streets, restaurants and shop, along with an open park and river promenade.

In March 2013, the historic district of New Castle became part of the several locations that form the First State National Monument, perhaps a prelude to the establishment of the State's first National Park, comprised of the Woodlawn Trust that preserved the vast green space of the Brandywine Valley.

The Old Courthouse (211 Delaware Street, Newcastle) is open to the public and contains a small museum.

ALONG THE COURSE OF BRANDYWINE CREEK

10 - BRANDYWINE CREEK

IN THE SOUTHEAST CORNER OF Lancaster County, Pennsylvania, is a 1,000 foot rise of the descending Piedmont called Welsh Mountain. The two branches of the Brandywine Creek flow out of Welsh Mountain, each formed within two miles of one another, in Honey Brook Township, Chester County.

The West and East Branches of the Brandywine flow parallel and southeast for some 30 miles. The two branches join to form Brandywine Creek 10 miles southeast of Coatesville. In another 21 meandering miles, along its course crossing the Delaware Arc, the Brandywine joins the Christiana River at Wilmington. The Christiana empties into the Delaware River.

The Brandywine Creek is one of the important waterways of the American Experience. It flows through the rich agricultural region of Chester County, known for its wheat production in the eighteenth and early nineteenth centuries. When industry was water-powered, it provided energy for some 150 mills over the course of three centuries, including a host of gristmills that produced Brandywine Superfine Flour, the powder works of the Du Pont Company at Hagley, and the Bancroft cotton mills and Walker's textile mill in Wilmington.

Just north of the Delaware Arc, Chadds Ford (through Howard Pyle) continues to be identified with the famous Brandywine School of Illustration of the turn of the century. Chadds Ford also was the home of three generations of Wyeths. The Brandywine River Museum in Chadds Ford honors a long and rich artistic tradition inspired by the beguiling landscape Around the Delaware Arc.

For many visitors, Chadds Ford sits at the center of the region Around the Delaware Arc.

The Battle of the Brandywine, the largest battle of the American Revolution, was fought in the Chadds Ford area. A remnant of Brandywine Battlefield remains, plus two houses that served as Washington's and Lafayette's respective headquarters.

The Brandywine Valley in Delaware remains significantly undeveloped thanks to numerous du Pont estates that have earned the area defined by Brandywine Creek the moniker of *Chateau Country.*

Brandywine Creek State Park (933 acres) includes two preserves: a stand of 190-year-old tulip trees and a fresh water marsh. As the Brandywine enters Delaware and flows toward Wilmington, more than 1000 acres along the Brandywine, established as the Rockford Woodlawn Trust by Bancroft interests, is now controlled by The Conservation Fund. In Wilmington, beneath the Market Street Bridge, Frederick Law Olmstead, in 1886, helped design the city's Brandywine Park along the Creek's more gently flowing waters.

The course of the Brandywine Creek attracts preservationists and conservationists. Today, Delaware interests seek a National Park around the Woodlawn property. Pennsylvania interests have proposed a Brandywine Creek Greenway from the sources of the East and West branches to the Delaware border.

The Lenni Lenape had at least three names for the Brandywine Creek: Wawaset, Sittacunck, and Tankopanican. (A variant of Wawaset is Wawassan, supposedly meaning "settling place of wild geese.") The name Brandywine most likely derives from an early Dutch settler named Brainende or Brantwyn.

11 - BRANDYWINE RIVER MUSEUM

IN 1973, AN ABANDONED MILL (Hoffman's Grist Mill, 1864) on the Brandywine Creek at Chadds Ford, Pennsylvania, was converted (by the Brandywine Conservancy) into an art museum to feature the art associated with the region Around the Delaware Arc.

Chadds Ford was the home of three generations of Wyeths, who had become America's most famous painting family: N.C. Wyeth father and grandfather, Andrew Wyeth son and father, and Jamie Wyeth son and grandson, plus other siblings of Andrew and their spouses. In the last quarter of the twentieth century, Andrew arguably became America's iconic artist. In addition to the museum's permanent of regional art, it also offers tours to N.C. Wyeth's house and studio, Andrew Wyeth's studio, and the Kuerner Farm where Andrew painted some 1,000 works, including his controversial Helga paintings.

The region Around the Delaware Arc had a host of nineteenth and twentieth century artists drawn to the distinctive landscape of Chester County and Northern Delaware. A robust school of illustration flourished in Chadds Ford and Wilmington at the turn of the century around Howard Pyle (1853-1911), illustrator and teacher. Pyle and his students, including N.C. Wyeth, later became known as the Brandywine School of Illustration. The region also was home to painters who specialized in portraiture and in still life, particularly of the *trompe l'oeil*, super-realistic style.

The Brandywine River Museum's permanent collection of some 3,000 pieces, while showcasing the Wyeths, also exhibits the other traditionally strong genres of the region: landscape, illustration, portraiture, still life, and *trompe l'oeil.* The museum stages frequent special exhibitions, many highlighting Brandywine Valley's regional art.

A dining room looks out to the Brandywine. A wildflower garden features native plants.

The Brandywine River Museum is located on U.S. Route 1 at Chadds Ford.

12 - N.C. WYETH HOUSE AND STUDIO

N.C. WYETH (1982-1945) AND HIS WIFE CAROLYN, bought (1911) 18 acres of land in Chadds Ford, Pennsylvania where they built a house and raised five talented children. N.C. had attended Howard Pyle's famous Chadds Ford summer school in 1902, becoming one of several successful protégés of the master illustrator. By 1903, Wyeth had his first commission. He famously illustrated an edition of *Treasure Island* in 1911, becoming a leading illustrator in a golden age of magazine and book illustrators. The proceeds from *Treasure Island* allowed him to purchase the Chadds Ford property.

His children Andrew, Henriette, and Carolyn became artists; Ann was an artist and composer; and Nathaniel C. was a prominent chemist.

N.C. died with a young grandson, in 1945, when, stalled on nearby railroad tracks, his car was hit by a slow-moving freight train. The odd and unexplainable circumstances of the accident raised questions about the nature of his relationship with his daughter-in-law and speculation that his grandson might be his son.

The Chadds Ford house where Wyeth and his wife raised their famous family and entertained celebrities of those between-wars days was occupied by his wife and then his daughter Carolyn, through her death in 1994.

The house, studio, and grounds became part of the Brandywine River Museum holdings after Carolyn's death. The museum, since 1996, offers tours to the N.C. Wyeth House and Studio as part of its program.

The house and studio retain much of the ambiance of the period when the Wyeths raised their children and N.C. painted. The studio houses costumes and other props that he used in his historical paintings. There are other memorable touches, such as the palette that remains as it was at his tragic death.

Those interested in experiencing more than just the paintings of the celebrated Wyeth clan of Chadds Ford has N.C. Wyeth's House and Studio as a particularly evocative starting point.

13 - ANDREW WYETH'S STUDIO

A N ARTIST'S STUDIO IS ALWAYS a treat to visit.

Andrew Wyeth's studio in Chadds Ford is particularly alluring, not just for the stature of the artist, but for the carefully recreated rooms that are true to how the Wyeths (Andrew, Betsy, and sons Nicholas and Jamie) used the space in the 1950s.

Originally, the 1875 schoolhouse was the Wyeth family home (1940-1961), as well as Andrew's original studio, a gift from N.C. Wyeth to his son and daughter-in law. From 1961 through 2008, Andrew used it exclusively as his Pennsylvania studio, where he painted many of his famous works, such as those associated with the Kuerner Farm, including the so-called Helga paintings. He even shared the studio for a few years (1961-1968) with his son Jamie.

The rooms are filled with signatures of Wyeth's life and career: family photographs, books and tin movie canisters, telephone numbers penciled on the wall, a Wawa egg carton remembering the egg tempera with which he painted—among a multitude of telling details. In the studio section, compelling disarray in the midst of which he worked spreads beneath a ceiling that appears to be peeling and threatens to fall.

For many visitors, this highly evocative, formerly sequestered place is a highlight of a visit to the Brandywine River Museum. The museum offers adjunct tours through the studio, permitting the visitor to ignore the sign that Andrew hand-lettered and hung on his door: "I am working, so please do not disturb. I do not sign autographs."

14 - THE KUERNER FARM

THE KUERNER FARM (ALSO RING Farm) is one of the places in Chadds Ford, Pennsylvania that is a must-see for those interested in the famous clan of artists, the Wyeths. It is included in the adjunct tours arranged by the Brandywine River Museum.

The Kuerner Farm physically touches the Battle of Brandywine. Its fields edge toward Brandywine Battlefield a half mile north. A cannonball and grapeshot were among Revolutionary artifacts found on the farm.

The current farmhouse was built in 1814 and added onto in 1850.

German immigrant Karl Kuerner and wife Anna rented the Ring Farm in 1926, buying it in 1940. They lived on the farm the rest of their lives, through his death in 1979 and hers in 1997. The Brandywine Conservancy bought it 1999. The Ring Farm is now better known as the Kuerner Farm.

The Kuerners associated mostly with fellow German immigrants. From his youth, Andrew befriended the Kuerners and they him (though Anna became increasingly reclusive). Karl regaled him with stories of the Black Forest region of Germany and combat during World War I.

Andrew Wyeth's first painting of the farm dates from 1932, when he was 15 years old. About a third of his life works (a 1,000 or so) relate to the Kuerner Farm. These works portray a number of themes and are in a variety of media.

In 1971, Andrew began to paint in secret Karl's caretaker Helga Testorf, a German immigrant. In 1987, 240 of the Helga paintings came to light and were exhibited. (Wyeth's friend Frolic Weymouth had hidden them away on his nearby Big Bend property.) These paintings, including nudes, caused a public controversy, and by report, unsettled Andrew's wife Betsy.

The Kuerner Farm has another association with the Wyeth family. It was on a railroad track at the northwest corner of the property that Andrew's father N.C. Wyeth and N.C.'s young grandson were killed (1945) in a stopped car by a slow moving freight train. The deaths remain a mystery but with a whiff of scandal: rumors immediately circulated that the grandson was actually N.C.'s own son fathered in an illicit affair with his daughter-in-law.

Andrew's Kuerner Farm landscapes lend themselves to psychological interpretations. His Helga paintings tease out variations of what *muse* means to an artist.

Kuerner farmhouse is located at 415 Ring Road, Chadds Ford, Pennsylvania.

15 - THE BRANDYWINE SCHOOL OF ILLUSTRATION

HOWARD PYLE (1853-1911) WAS BORN IN Wilmington, Delaware. He became a pivotal figure in the cultural/artistic lore of the region Around the Delaware Arc. In fact, his role as teacher and founding figure of the so-called Brandywine School of Illustration resonates today in Chadds Ford through the legacy of the Wyeth family and the region's artistic shrine, the Brandywine River Museum.

Pyle had scant formal training, only a couple of years of study in a Philadelphia artist's studio and a few classes at the Arts Student League of New York. Otherwise, he taught himself, while developing a distinctive style of illustration.

He sold his first illustration in 1878 to *Scribner's Magazine*. Success followed in magazine work and then in book illustration, beginning with a now monumental 1883 edition of *The Merry Adventures of Robin Hood*. (Commentators conclude Pyle single-handedly defined the "pirate costume" with puffy shirt and sashed pants, swashbuckler boot, head, scarf, over-brimmed hat, and such.)

Pyle also wrote his own historical themed books. His prose, as well as his illustration appealed to children and youth. He played a significant role in a revival of children's literature. His art exploded with drama, where the imagination blended realism's eye for detail with romanticism's larger than life, mythic qualities.

He taught illustration at the Drexel Institute from 1894 through 1900. During that era, for five consecutive summers after 1898, he led a summer school in the old Chadds Ford Turner's mill, inviting only the best students. A few became the best-known illustrators/artists of the turn of the century.

A charming newspaper article of the day described Pyle's summer school: "The studio work room is an old ivy-covered mill, within whose cool and shaded walls there still clings an odor of grain. Here the 'ten' work each day from 8 o'clock until 5, long hours for summer time, when any work drags. When the day's work is ended - and they know that time by the tinkle of bells of the homecoming cows - they wash their brushes in a neighboring stream, stow away their painting paraphernalia behind doors and on shelves, mount their bicycles and disperse for the night. The men of the school lodge at a small country hotel in Chadd's Ford, and the girls keep house in a quaint old farm house, used long ago as Lafayette's headquarters during the Battle of Brandywine."

The Brandywine Group under Pyle's influence included Frank Schoonover, Maxfield Parrish, and of course, N.C. Wyeth, who eventually settled in Chadds Ford and raised a family of artists through three generations.

Why did Pyle choose Chadds Ford? He knew it through his Wilmington connection. With a station along the Brandywine, there was easy access by railroad to Philadelphia and Wilmington. The inspiring landscape steeped in rural solitude, as well as charm, was the ultimate recommendation.

Pyle's sudden death in 1911 had direct ties to a core collection of a hundred of his works that ultimately resulted in the founding of the Delaware Art Museum (Wilmington). The Museum has a fine collection of his luminous paintings on permanent display.

16 - *THREE COLONIAL BUILDINGS*

A TRIO OF CHESTER COUNTY, Pennsylvania buildings, erected in the early decades of the eighteenth century, were part of the landscape of the Battle of Brandywine (1777). Restored and furnished with period pieces, these buildings supplement Washington's Headquarters (Ring House) and Lafayette's Headquarters (Gilpin House) on the grounds of the Brandywine Battlefield Historic Site near Chadds Ford.

The oldest of these now-public buildings is the William Brinton House, erected in 1704, on a country road in Delaware County, Pennsylvania just south of West Chester (21 Oakland Road). Near busy and congested Route 202, it sits in a surprisingly serene setting. It represents English Quaker buildings of the region and era. It has been carefully furnished with period furniture. The site includes a handsome barn and open grounds.

In 1714, John Barns built a residence on what is now Route 1, the Baltimore Pike. In the colonial era, this was a main route between Pennsylvania and Maryland. Barns operated it as a tavern (1722 to 1731) on "ye Good Road to Nottingham." Barns advertised "ye accommodation of Man and Horse."

A grandson of William Brinton bought the property in 1753. It remained in the Brinton family for a hundred years. The Chadds Ford Historical Society bought the building in 1968, restoring and furnishing it as a country tavern of the era. The interior has many features dating from its original construction. An eighteenth century cooking garden is planted on its modest grounds. The Barns-Brinton House features open-hearth cooking. When Route 1 was rerouted a little to the north in 1938, the original front of the house no longer faced the highway.

The John Chad House dates from 1725. It is located a mile and a half from the Barns-Brinton House, on Old Route 100, now Creek Road. Chad, in addition to farming, operated (1731-1760) a ferry on the Brandywine Creek. Hence, the nearby village became known as Chadds Ford. A simple fieldstone structure, representative of colonial Quaker architecture, it is built into a hill above the Creek's flood plain. It was also purchased in 1968 by the Chadds Ford Historical Society, which restored and furnished it to the period of John Chad. Its interior features original woodwork, including oak floors.

Reputedly, Chad's widow Elizabeth, from an attic window, watched the movement of troops during the Battle of the Brandywine.

17 - Battle of Brandywine Creek

IT WAS IN THE EARLY months of the second year of the Revolutionary War. The British were occupying New York City and their next objective was Philadelphia, in hopes of splitting the rebel colonies asunder.

Toward summer's end in 1777, a flotilla of British ships transported some 17,000 troops and supplies south to the Chesapeake and the head of the Elk River, near Elkton, Maryland. Philadelphia lay 40 some miles to the north. The most direct route from Elkton to Philadelphia followed the Baltimore Pike (today's Route 1). To repel the British, 20,000 Colonial troops under George Washington's command assembled south of Philadelphia.

The concentration of troops around Chadds Ford on the day of the battle—upwards of 30,000 Colonials and British—was the largest during the war. The main battle lasted only a day (September 11, 1777).

A brief engagement at Chadds Ford caused the British to call for reinforcements, as they retreated to the walls of the nearby Quaker Meeting House (Old Kennett Meeting). During this early engagement, General Howe's British troops out-flanked General Washington's Colonials.

The battle moved north another three miles to the hills of the current Brandywine Battlefield State Park. Skirmishes took place along the right flank, near the grounds of another Quaker Meeting House at Birmingham, a mile north of Chadds Ford.

When the center weakened and with the flanks under attack, contingents of the Continental Army began an orderly retreat. By evening, the entire Continental Army was on its way to Chester on the Delaware River south of Philadelphia.

General Howe's official report of the battle claimed Colonial losses totaled 300 killed, 600 wounded, and 400 captured. Among the uncaptured wounded, was the young French General Lafayette, fighting his first battle. Despite the wound, Lafayette helped organize the retreat.

The British soon entered Philadelphia without further resistance. They occupied the city (September 26, 1777). The Continental Congress fled to Lancaster (for a day) and then to York. The Colonial Army would winter at Valley Forge.

Though the battle was lost and General Washington admitted he made strategic mistakes, contemporary apologists maintain that the Colonials proved their mettle.

The Brandywine Battlefield Site on Route 1 has two significant structures dating to 1777, known as Washington and Lafayette's headquarters, respectively the Ring and the Gilpin Houses. Other pertinent sites, including the two Quaker Meeting Houses at Kennett and Birmingham are still standing. Birmingham Meeting's graveyard interred American, British, and Hessian combatants.

Nearby landscapes of The Battlefield of the Brandywine (Meeting House Road, West Chester) has walking trails traversing a rolling landscape that carries the imagination back to the day of the largest battle of the Revolutionary War.

18 - The Peace Garden at Birmingham

Outside of West Chester on Birmingham Road is the meeting house of the Birmingham Friends Meeting, organized in 1690. A log meeting house was first erected on the site in 1722. A log school was added to the grounds in 1756. The current stone building was built in 1763 and enlarged in 1818. The log schoolhouse was replaced the following year with a memorable octagonal building that survives.

The historic school building now houses The Peace Center at Birmingham, a cooperative effort of the nonsectarian Chester County Peace Movement and the Birmingham Friends Quaker Meeting.

The Peace Garden honors Quaker pacifism generally, while specifically remembering the Battle of Brandywine fought on September 11, 1777, the largest concentration of troops in the

Revolutionary War. Before the battle, the Meeting House served as a hospital for Continental soldiers. During the battle, the burial ground walls provided cover for Continental soldiers being flanked by British troops.

After driving the Continental army toward Philadelphia, the British used the Meeting House for a hospital for their wounded soldiers. Scores of Continental and British combatants (including German mercenaries) were buried in a common grave within the Meeting House cemetery.

Today, within the same burial ground walls, there is a meaningful Peace Garden, planted with native flowers and grasses.

A marker on the site declares: "During the Battle of the Brandywine on September 11, 1777, the American Army used the walls of this Quaker Burial Ground in their first line of defense. Both armies used this meetinghouse of Quaker pacifists as a hospital. Behind the wall is the common grave of British and American soldiers killed in the battle.

"The Peace Garden at Birmingham surrounding this grave is a place to contemplate a world without war. This site is dedicated to the imperative need to employ peaceful alternatives to deadly conflict."

The Peace Garden is unassuming: a standing marker as a focus with an arc of flat stones engraved with peace quotations, a few encircling benches, a low wall-enclosed lawn and old trees keeping sentinel over what is arguably a sacred site of the American experience.

The Birmingham Meeting House is located at 1245 Birmingham Road, West Chester, PA

19 - CHRIS SANDERSON MUSEUM

IN CHADDS FORD VILLAGE, IN a small white house on old Route 100 (Creek Road), is a curious museum, the depository of the lifelong collecting of Chester County resident Chris Sanderson (1882-1966).

Educated at the West Chester Normal School, Sanderson was a schoolteacher and principle. He had an avocation for local history and lore. With his mother, he once lived at the Ring House (Washington's Headquarters) on what is now the Brandywine Battlefield Park. He was a collector of historical objects and contemporary memorabilia. He first spoke on radio in 1923. He had a ten-year show on WDEL called "Historic Rambles." He lectured on a variety of subjects, often on the Battle of Brandywine about which he was a local authority. He dabbled in local acting and writing poetry. Trained on the violin, Sanderson was a fiddler who promoted old time fiddling; he played and called at local square dances with his Pocopson Valley Boys. He was a friend of the Wyeth family and posed for both N.C. and Andy. The latter painted an engaging winter scene portrait of Sanderson. Sanderson never drove a car and relied on the kindness of strangers, as he hitchhiked wherever he needed to go, often with his fiddle and briefcase in tow. Above all he was a collector.

When he died, Sanderson's modest house was chock-full of the stuff he had collected throughout his lifetime. Appearances suggest that he was a hoarder. Friends, who viewed the interior of the house after he died, attested that much of what it contained looked like trash; the house was totally unkempt. However, one acquaintance, Tommy Thompson, saw potential and saved Sanderson's stuff from being simply thrown out. A prescient local board (including Andrew Wyeth) set about creating a foundation and museum. It took a year and a half to simply sort through Sanderson's accumulation of stuff.

The museum is now well organized, though nearly overwhelming in its crowded displays compounded by the house's small rooms. In aggregate, the collection relates to the eccentric and iconic twentieth century Chadds Ford resident Chris Sanderson, who had an obvious affection for the region Around the Delaware Arc. Perhaps better than any other local institution, Sanderson's collection conveys, in the extreme, the "love of place" as well as the "influence of place" have on its residents.

The Chris Sanderson Museum is a good place to visit at the beginning or the end—prelude or postlude—while exploring the region Around the Delaware Arc, particularly when visiting Chadds Ford.

It is a convenient means to comprehend the powerful affect that landscape and history create for visitor or resident of the Brandywine region. What on the surface may appear to be the eccentric Museum's weakness may very well be its strength, for the visitor willing to take the time and effort to engage and imagine.

The Chris Sanderson Museum is located at 1755 Creek Road (Old Route 100), Chadds Ford.

20 - LAFAYETTE'S SYCAMORE

ADJACENT TO THE HANDSOME GILPIN Farm House (also known as Lafayette's Headquarters) at the Brandywine Battlefield site (along Route 1 mile east of Chadds Ford) stands a huge sycamore tree. It was a large tree in 1777, large enough to shelter Colonial soldiers. Over centuries of standing in open space, perched on rising land, the tree has risen and spread to become a handsome and compelling specimen of its kind.

Sycamores are one of the trees that characterize the region Around the Delaware Arc, lining the banks of creeks flowing from Pennsylvania into Delaware, notably the picturesque Brandywine Creek. They are distinctive because of their mottled bark—patches of rough gray and smooth tan with tones of green. (To the modern eye it resembles camouflage.) Arguably, sycamores are the easiest to identify of all local trees.

In the long history of the Brandywine inspired artists, a sycamore often had a prominent place in their canvases. An example is Andrew Wyeth's "Sycamore Tree and Hunter" (1943) that also served as a memorable cover for a Saturday Evening Post magazine.

The great tree at the Brandywine Battlefield, because it sheltered soldiers during the battle, established the notion that sycamores symbolize *protection*.

Legend incorrectly maintained that Lafayette had his battle wound dressed beneath the tree. (Brandywine was the 20-year-old general's first battle.) Lafayette visited the farmhouse and tree during a triumphant 1824 tour of America.

For the region Around the Delaware Arc, the Lafayette sycamore is an *axis mundi/world tree*.

COUNTRY ESTATE MOVEMENT

21 - CHATEAU COUNTRY

FROM WILMINGTON, DELAWARE INTO SOUTHERN Chester County, Pennsylvania, generally following the course of Brandywine Creek is the so-called "Chateau Country," identified by twentieth century estates and country homes of the du Pont family.

Route 52 (Kennett Pike) is the main artery through Chateau Country. It was originally a toll road. Pierre S. du Pont (then president of the family Company), bought and improved the toll road to provide better access from company headquarters in Wilmington to his country estate known as Longwood. When completed, he sold it to the State for a dollar.

The literal and figurative fortunes of the du Pont family made a great shift in the early twentieth century. Three first cousins, Alfred I. du Pont, Pierre S. du Pont, and T. Coleman du Pont, joined together to buy (1901) the du Pont Powder company that the old family partnership no longer wanted to own and operate. After the sale, the Du Pont Company diversified its products. Simultaneously, a younger generation began to live a more lavish, though sequestered style of life, manifested in the building of country estates. These huge properties were often named after chateaus in France where the du Pont family had originated.

An extreme example of the du Pont country manor houses was Winterthur. After inheriting it in 1926, Henry Francis du Pont transformed the family home from 30 rooms to 175 rooms, creating tableaus of rooms with period American furnishings. The whirlwind project was completed in 1932. Winterthur is now an important museum of Americana with accompanying gardens and library off Route 52.

Farther north along the Kennett Pike into Pennsylvania is Pierre S. du Pont's Longwood. He purchased the property in 1906, ostensibly to save a well-established arboretum known as Peirce's Park. He added to the buildings and grounds through the 1930s. Upon his death in 1946, Longwood was left to a foundation to preserve the conservatories and gardens for the public's pleasure.

Alfred I. du Pont's great estate outside of the city of Wilmington, Nemours, was built by the most controversial of the three cousins. Begun in 1907, designed in a late-18th-century French style, Nemours sat on 3,000 acres, surrounded by nine-foot tall granite walls studded with many colored shards of glass. From that original estate, 300 acres of the original chateau with formal French gardens survive intact and may be visited. The remainder of the old estate is part of a world famous children's hospital.

Other du Pont country estates include, Mt. Cuba built (1935) by Lammot du Pont Copeland, in the style of a Colonial revival manor house. The estate is now a 600-acre horticulture center open to the public. The most visible, since it is perched on the top of a hill surrounded by open fields, Granogue (1923), sits on land purchased by Irénée DuPont in 1921. It is now owned by Irénée du Pont Jr. It remains a private estate.

The relatively undeveloped but open nature of the Brandywine Valley, accessed from winding roads, rising and falling among picturesque Piedmont hills, while crossing tumbling streams that merge with the celebrated Brandywine Creek, can readily be attributed to such du Pont estates. Their great tracts of land preserved the Valley from development during the post-World War II era, when Wilmington expanded in all other directions.

Several of the du Pont Country Estates are maintained by foundations that preserve the large tracts and allow limited public access to grounds.

22 - Kennett Pike

William What is now Delaware Route 52 is one of two branches (with Route 100) of a designated National Scenic Byway (Brandywine Valley Byway, 2005) that runs from the heart of Wilmington north to the Delaware Arc.

In 1810, New Castle County commissioned a survey for the best route from Wilmington through Centreville and beyond to the state line. In 1811, Delaware granted a charter to The Wilmington and Kennett Turnpike Company. For 30,000 dollars the Company built a hard-surface, two lane road with a 100-foot right of way. Completed in 1814, the turnpike prospered through the post-Civil War era.

During his tenure as company president (1915-1919), Pierre S. du Pont's estate Longwood, located in Kennett Square, Pennsylvania, was a hard drive from du Pont's Wilmington office in 1919, after the War, Pierre bought out the Wilmington and Kennett Turnpike Company's shareholders at double par value and assumed some $10,000 in accumulated debt.

Once du Pont owned it, he widened the route to its chartered 100 feet, paved the two lanes, and when it was completed in 1920, transferred the title to the State for the consideration of one dollar. Pierre did put certain restrictions on the deed of transfer, including "no trolley cars shall be permitted; no advertising signs are to be erected or maintained upon or along the road, without receiving the consent of each and every property owner along its entire length."

In 1957, The Kennett Pike Association, a citizen's group, formed to limit development and preserve "the values and beauty indigenous to Christiana Hundred" along the route of the Kennett Pike."

Route 52 passes through Greenville, Winterthur, and Centerville. Along or near the route are 12 major du Pont family estates, including the "big three:" Nemours and Winterthur in Delaware and, a little into Pennsylvania, Longwood.

23 - LONGWOOD GARDENS

IN 1906, PIERRE S. DU PONT (1870-1954) bought the Peirce property at Longwood, Chester County, Pennsylvania, just north of where Route 52 (Kennett Pike) crosses the Delaware Arc. In the spirit of the era and of the du Pont family, he transformed Longwood into a country manor estate.

He retreated to Longwood on the weekends. To ease his 11 mile ride to and from Wilmington, he bought the old Kennett Pike (Route 52, 1919), paved it, and sold it to the State (for a dollar) to keep and maintain.

In 1701, Quaker James Peirce bought 500 acres near Kennett Square from William Penn. The land passed through generations of Peirces, who called it Evergreen Glade. The Peirce family planted an arboretum in 1798, which by the mid-nineteenth century became one of the finest arboreta in the nation, as well as an early public park. The grounds were known as Peirce's Park.

The place acquired the name Longwood in the tumultuous years before the Civil War, from a stretch of forest through which fugitive slaves passed as they entered freedom in Pennsylvania. (Longwood had a local Quaker Meeting House, with Friends active in assisting fugitive slaves.)

In 1906, when the arboretum was threatened with being razed, on a whim, du Pont purchased the property.

In 1907, du Pont planted a 600-foot-long Flower Garden Walk. In 1909, he held his first Garden Party to such success that he thereafter sought more sumptuous garden settings for his annual summer fete. In 1914, he hosted the first performance in a new outdoor theater. He enlarged the original Peirce house into a country manor with certain amenities, including a bowling alley and a small conservatory. He was next inspired to build a grand conservatory with pipe organ that was completed in 1921. (The organ would later triple in size. He claimed that he built for his hard-of-hearing wife, so she might enjoy music.) His attention turned to fountains, which were built throughout the estate in the 1930s, including the Main Fountain Garden in front of the Conservatory. Its 10,000 gallons a minute shot as high as 130 feet and was illuminated in various colors. In 1930, he installed a carillon atop a 61-foot tower. His final large project in 1939 was a huge 30-by-36-foot oval analemmatic sundial now standing in the Topiary Garden, accurate to two minutes.

At Longwood, du Pont melded the technology of the great world fairs he had attended, stimulating his love of technology, with his broad-ranging aesthetics that included horticulture, theater, and music.

In 1937, Pierre established a charitable foundation. In 1946, Longwood Gardens was turned over to the foundation. Pierre S. du Pont died in 1954, his estate further endowing Longwood Gardens. Since then, Longwood Gardens has grown to rank among the world's best-known horticultural displays.

Longwood Gardens sits in the midst of more than a thousand acres, a third accessible to visitors. There are twenty outdoor gardens and twenty indoor gardens. The indoor gardens are contained within four and a half acres of heated and covered conservatories. In total, the grounds host some 11,000 varieties of plants.

Longwood Gardens is located at 1001 Longwood Rd, Kennett Square, Pennsylvania.

Horticultural Hall, Longwood Gardens, near Wilmington, Delaware

24 - WINTERTHUR

IT IS UNIMAGINABLE THAT ANY account of what to visit Around the Delaware Arc would not include the du Pont estate of Henry Francis (H.F.) du Pont (1880-1969): Winterthur.

The house (referred to today as The Museum) on this site when H.F. was born had 30 rooms. (Before the Civil War, it had been a mere 12-room Greek Revival country home.) He added another 145 rooms during his lifetime. Today, a massive manor house sits on a thousand preserved acres on a rolling landscape with several natural gardens.

H.F. studied horticulture at Harvard. After his father (Henry A., 1838-1926) became a United States Senator (1906), young Henry took over the supervision of the gardens, some 60 acres around the house that progressed from formal into natural tableaus as the flowers approached the surrounding fields. The Senator (he was known as Colonel from his Civil War rank) had a formidable presence. As a young man, in the du Pont pantheon, H.F. appeared to be a timid failure. Indeed, he had an almost debilitating "nervous" condition. His larger-than-life father did not expect much from him.

By 1914, H.F. was supervising the entire estate. After his father's death, H.F. expanded the home, gardens, and land. Over his lifetime, the younger du Pont transformed Winterthur into a mind-boggling estate surrounded by 2500 acres of sculptured Piedmont landscape.

H.F. developed a passion for American decorative arts, following his 1916 marriage. He became a collector of Americana from the seventeenth through the mid-nineteenth centuries. He decorated room after room with period treasures from his ample resources, much of it munitions money derived from World War I, from which the du Ponts had profited handsomely. (By the 1930s, the du Ponts, were being castigated as Merchants of Death and the Company was under Congressional investigation for war profiteering.)

Some art critics called the interior of Winterthur a rabbit warren of rooms accommodating an indiscriminate hodgepodge of period decorations. The estate's pretensions and fussy ways of its owner reputedly put off fellow du Ponts.

H.F. also became a famous breeder of Holstein-Friesian cattle and had a fine flock of Dorset sheep. The estate housed a variety of other prime domestic animals, manicured flower and vegetable gardens, greenhouses, sawmill, and a little town complete with a railroad station and a post office. A retinue of some 250 varied workers maintained Winterthur.

In 1951, H.F. du Pont established the Winterthur Museum and Country Estate, opening the mansion and gardens to the public. The Museum is frequently cited as the finest museum of the decorative arts in the world. The collection has 90,000 pieces of Americana spanning two centuries: 1640-1840.

Winterthur bears witness to early twentieth century wealth and its privileges, as well as Henry Francis du Pont's personality. About half of the estate, 933 acres, called a "dairy farm," was sold to the State in 1965, becoming Brandywine Creek State Park.

Winterthur is located six miles north of Wilmington on 5105 Kennett Pike (Route 52) in Winterthur, Delaware.

25 - Low Granite Walls

IN THE 1970S, A NEW way of thinking about geography emerged, as geographers began to look at the emotional connections between physical environment and human beings. An important cultural geographer, Yi-Fu Tuan used the word *topophilia* (love of place) to describe such emotional connections.

The region Around the Delaware Arc is a particularly apt landscape to apply the insights of what is called humanist geography.

One of the basic distinctions humanist geographers make is between *carpentered* and *noncarpentered* places. The latter relates to Nature and natural landscapes. *Carpentered* implies the activity of human beings and is observed through straight lines, angles, and rectangular shapes.

The region Around the Delaware Arc is a contrast between the Piedmont's tumbling hills, flowing streams, a hodgepodge of trees blending to a forest, and protruding rock veneered with 300 plus years of human activity suited to the resources at hand. Houses, barns, mills, fields, and even roads, such as the turnpikes of the Colonial era, though of and from the land, imposed a linear order on an undulating natural landscape.

As preservationists and conservationists seek to limit development and keep green space, there is the background of generations of human effect worth pondering. For example, consider the Chateau Country with its grand country manors and open fields. Often, following the rising and falling hills, low stone walls using locally quarried granite, define boundaries that mutely limit public access. Yet it is also obvious many walls were obviously imposed for aesthetic effect.

Reputedly, the owner of Winterthur, Henry A. du Pont (1838-1926) known as Colonel for his rank in the Union Army during the Civil War, who was also a turn of the century conservative United State Senator, conceived the notion of such walls. While riding with his two greyhounds, he imagined stone walls defining his estate, as well as the estates of the other du Ponts. These are not functional; rather, they are decorative walls. Historians conclude that such walls are the most visible relics of company labor used on private du Pont estate.

Local legend says that the masons (many of Italian descent) the Du Pont Company retained to build and repair the Powder Works on the Brandywine (that occasionally exploded) were also used to build handsome, decorative boundary walls around and through individual family estates. (In 1921, the Du Pont Company ended its powder making on the Brandywine and the masons, among other trades, were left to their own resources.)

Today, these undulating blue granite walls evoke ambivalent feelings, depending on orientation and aesthetic, as well as knowledge of the viewer. But invariably they do arouse feelings.

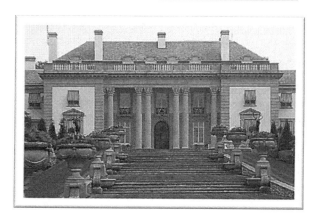

26 - NEMOURS

ARGUABLY, THE MOST JAW-DROPPING of all the du Pont country manors and estates is Nemours House and Gardens located north of downtown Wilmington, Delaware. The mansion was built in 1909-1910 by Alfred I. Du Pont (1864-1935), a chateau cast in a French classical style (Louis XVI-Rococo). The house is decorated lavishly with museum quality furniture and artwork. The estate has a host of formal French (Versailles inspired) and Italian gardens: The Boxwood Garden, The Reflecting Pool, The Colonnade, The Sunken Gardens, and The Temple of Love. The grounds have many fountains and statues, a carillon, and naturalized wooded areas. The entire estate is bounded by an imposing nine-foot granite wall, its top embedded with shards of vary-colored glass.

Three backstories help a visitor better understand what Nemours represents: The first involves the Country Estate Movement of the turn of the century, by which wealthy industrialists legitimized their wealth by affecting the lifestyle of country gentry. For the estate's name, Alfred reached back in time and across the Atlantic to a French town of the du Pont family's origin: Nemours

The second backstory involves the internal politics and machinations of the Du Pont Company/du Pont family. On the brink of the Company being sold to a competitor, three cousins Pierre S., Thomas Coleman, and Alfred I. had maneuvered a different sort of Company with a 1902 buyout of the old family's powder/explosives business.

Pierre and Alfred disagreed about the running of the revamped company. In 1911, Alfred was unceremoniously squeezed out, at least in part, because his du Pont relatives were scandalized by his private behavior.

The third backstory relates to Alfred's love and marital interests. He won his first wife Bessie (a second cousin) from a brother, marrying her in 1887. As a consequence, the brother killed himself with a single shot to the head. Alfred and Bessie had four children and occupied a rambling Victoria mansion (Swamp Hall, his childhood home) near the powder works on the Brandywine. Alfred divorced Bessie in 1906, and within two months (1907) married Mary (Alicia) Hayward Bradford (a second cousin). Bessie and Alicia were first cousins.

Alicia Bradford had been married to George Amory Maddox, Alfred's secretary. Later suspicions speculated that Alfred finagled the marriage. The Maddox's lived near the du Ponts. Alicia took trips to New York City, ostensibly to visit family, at the same time Alfred was there doing business. It seemed clear, particularly to family members, that Maddox was a "beard," especially when the Maddox's sole child, a daughter strongly resembled Alfred. When Alfred married Alicia, he adopted the daughter, also named Alicia. Then, in a 1910 *coup de grace*, he evicted his first wife and family from "The Swamp" and had the building razed. The du Pont women took pains to shun Alfred and Alicia.

Thus, Nemours, built by Alfred for Alicia, was an in-your-face declaration, perhaps to the world, but surely to the family. The prominent Temple of Love might be viewed in this light.

The house, furnishings, and grounds of the estate recently underwent a $39 million, three-year renovation.

The public entrance to Nemours is 1600 Rockland Road, Wilmington, Delaware.

27 - SHARDS OF GLASS

NEMOURS MANSION AND ESTATE IS one of the most celebrated for it lavishness among several du Pont country mansions and manor houses built in the first two decades of the twentieth century Around the Delaware Arc. Nemours, with a 45,000 square interior, was the home of Alfred I. du Pont, one of the three cousins who bought the family company in 1901 and transformed it into a diversified and exceedingly successful corporation.

Alfred had already scandalized the extended, conservative du Pont family, when he "stole" a younger brother's girlfriend, Bessie, to be his wife. The brother committed suicide with a shot to the head. Married to Bessie Gardner, who was also his cousin, Alfred had four children and at least one affair, with a cousin, also named Alicia. Alfred divorced Bessie and married Alicia. He adopted her daughter, who many suspected was Alfred's daughter, too. The family effectively shunned the newly married couple. Alfred built Nemours for Alicia on a 3,000-acre estate in 1909-1910. The family ganged together and "fired" Alfred in 1912.

A prominent feature of the estate for the locals is a nine-foot gray granite wall that surrounds the vast grounds, shrouding the estate from public view. If the wall were not sufficient by itself, embedded on top were multi-hued shards of glass. Why the glass?

Speculation abounded, converging into two legends. The first legend contended that the ominous wall crowned with shimmering broken glass was intended to keep out Alfred's fellow du Pont family members—their mutual animosity was so great. The second legend contended that the du Pont family's proclivity to marry cousins resulted in a number of physically and emotionally disabled progeny. In this regard, the wall kept the *hoi polloi* from viewing these disabled children and their nurses. Both versions fed into the du Pont family mythic story.

The truth may be as simple as the glass-topped walls were erected in imitation of French country manors after which Alfred styled Nemours.

A century later, many of the glass shards remain to keep alive old speculations.

28 - BLUE BALL BARN

A PIECE OF THE ONGOING story of life Around the Delaware Arc involves preservation. What of the surviving three hundred years of history is worth preserving?

This issue surfaced when Delaware Routes 202 and 141 went through redesign in the early years of the 2000s. As part of the project, the State of Delaware decided to improve 225 acres at this intersection, including a remnant dairy barn, once part of Alfred I. du Pont's Nemours estate.

Built in 1914, the barn fit into the notions of the Country Estate Movement, by which wealthy industrialists and businessmen built manor-like houses on large tracts of land. The land was often farmed, lending the air of country gentleman to their owners, who became facsimile landed gentry.

Alfred I. Du Pont, who was an innovative scientist/technician for the family Company, created a state of the art dairy barn, with smooth, easy to clean surfaces, room for a herd of cows, with the upper level a storage area for grains and other feed. Ostensibly, the dairy provided for his nearby estate of Nemours. It was an active farm for Nemours through the early 1940s, after which it was rented to a tenant farmer.

In 1971, the Nemours company told its tenant to cease farming, quickly tearing down all buildings except the dairy complex. This is the building the State incorporated as the focal point of its 225-acre Alapocas State Park.

While the barn and adjoining dairy represented the consolidation and expansion of farming in the early twentieth century, as well as a state of the art modern dairy barn, the barn on its own architectural merits was not all that extraordinary. But it did have the du Pont imprimatur and stood in the midst of surrounding parkland. It was cunningly preserved and meaningfully repurposed.

Today, it houses the Delaware Folk Art Collection and is a handsome venue for a host of activities.

The original architectural elements of the barn are visible, but the overall remodeling has transformed the building into a contemporary space with plenty of light and open space.

The Blue Ball Barn, repurposed into a museum and public space, is an example how preservation and innovation work hand in hand on sites throughout the region Around the Delaware Arc. (Consider the Brandywine Museum built around a nineteenth century Chadds Ford gristmill.)

The name Blue Ball derives from an early tavern along the old Wilmington Pike and its custom of displaying a blue painted ball on a post to signify that a passenger for the passing stage waited inside the inn. Throughout the twentieth century, a blue ball on a post at the site was a familiar sight.

The entrance to Blue Ball Barn is 1914 West Park Drive, Wilmington.

29 - MT. CUBA CENTER

M<small>T. CUBA CENTER IS A</small> 600 acre former estate of Lammot du Pont Copeland (1905-1983), who served as president of the Du Pont Company from 1962 to 1967. The private property is midway between Hockessin and Greenville, Delaware. He and his wife Pamela Cunningham Copeland built their Colonial Revival manor house in 1937. Sharing a passion for gardens and plants, they transformed the Piedmont landscape of their secluded estate.

A prominent Philadelphia landscape architect Thomas W. Sears designed the formal gardens around the house. Marian Cruger Coffin, a pioneering landscape architect, designed the Round Garden in 1949. Landscape architect Seth Kelsey began the development of woodland and wildflower gardens that featured native plants, constructed ponds, and walkways. The Copelands were anticipating that someday their estate would be open to the public as a proposed Mount Cuba Botanical Park.

After Kelsey left in 1970, under the influence of University of Delaware horticulturalist Richard W. Lighty, the Copelands changed their strategy and began to focus on plants native to this part of the Piedmont. In 1983, Lighty became the first director of Mt. Cuba Center.

Today the gardens are noted for their native plantings on a picturesque landscape of open space and forest. It features East Coast Piedmont plants and boasts of 4,600 accessions representing more than 1,800 taxa. It is lauded as the Mid-Atlantic region's premier site for native plants.

The gardens of Mt. Cuba Center, maintained by a not-for profit foundation, have been inaccessible except for one day a year and for pre-arranged tours of small groups. Now the gardens are open on Fridays and Saturdays for those who wish to stroll the garden paths.

By becoming more public, the Mt. Cuba Center hopes to better fulfill Mrs. Lammot du Pont Copeland's stated legacy: "I want this to be a place where people will learn to appreciate our native plants and to see how these plants can enrich their lives so that they, in turn, will become conservators of our natural habitats." (She died in 2001).

In addition to adapting to younger generations plus horticulture and environmental education, Mt. Cuba Center is leading an initiative to create Delaware's first national park. Mt. Cuba donated 20 million dollars to the Conservation Fund to purchase the Woodlawn Trust lands in anticipation of a Brandywine Valley National Park.

Access Mt. Cuba Center via 3120 Barley Mill Road, Hockessin, Delaware.

30 - BELLEVUE HALL

N EAR THE DELAWARE RIVER, SOUTH of Claymont, the former Bellevue Hall estate (William du Pont, *pere et fils*) is now a Delaware State Park.

The senior du Pont (1855-1928) bought the property in 1883. The house already on the property resembled a medieval castle, known as Woolton Hall. He added additional property and buildings, while transforming the medieval castle into a facsimile of Montpelier (Dolley and James Madison's Virginia estate). He already owned the real Montpelier.

The junior du Pont was raised in the Virginia Montpelier, where his lifelong affair with horses began. When he inherited Bellevue Hall, he transformed the grounds to accommodate breeding barns and stable, a full scale racetrack, and other training facilities for the horses he loved. He built gardens and added a pond. He also built tennis courts (including an indoor court) and other training facilities for his second wife (1947), top ranked tennis professional Margaret Osborne.

William du Pont Jr. was one of the prominent horsemen of the twentieth century. He and his first wife Jean owned Liseter Hall Farm in Newtown, Pennsylvania and raced under the name of Foxcatcher Farm. He developed a 5,000-acre equestrian facility at Fair Hill, Maryland. He also designed more than a score of racetracks, including Delaware Park, after lobbying the State for parimutuel gambling.

When the junior du Pont died in 1965, his heirs had no interest in keeping the Bellevue Hall property. Perhaps the neighborhood had become too déclassé. The back of Bellevue Hall is within a few hundred yards of busy and very common Philadelphia Pike (Route 13).

The State of Delaware bought the entire 328-acre estate in 1976 and turned it into a multi-use state park. The barn complex adjacent to the main house needs attention, but the touch of neglect/decay adds to air of changing tastes and fortunes of such once-grand country manor estates.

Of particular note is an arboretum of more than seventy mature trees that surround the great house. Markers identify the trees. The paved walkway permits visitors to leisurely and with little effort experience local and exotic trees in a manicured landscape.

Bellevue Hall is located at 911 Philadelphia Pike, Wilmington.

31 – GIBRALTAR

ON GREENHILL AND PENNSYLVANIA AVENUES, Wilmington, Delaware, contained within high granite walls, sits an abandoned du Pont family estate, named Gibraltar. The house and grounds, constructed of Brandywine granite, commands one of the highest elevations in the city—a rocky outcropping.

From 1844 through 1909, the John Rodney Brinckle family (relatives to Caesar Rodney) lived in the original Italianate mansion on six acres, in the neighborhood known as the Highlands.

In 1909, during the era of the American Country Estate Movement, Hugh Rodney Sharp and Isabella Mathieu du Pont Sharp bought the property. In 1915, the Sharps began in to renovate and expand the house and the grounds.

The best-known feature of this country manor estate was formal gardens designed between 1916 and 1923 by Marian Cruger Coffin, a pioneering and successful female landscape architect. (She came with the recommendation of her friend Henry Francis du Pont of Winterthur.) Her design features at Gibraltar included several "garden rooms," descending terraces integrated into the outdoor gardens, adding outdoor attributes to the house and its setting. The terraced "garden rooms" were connected by a monumental, curving marble staircase.

H. Rodney Sharp was an early and important Delaware preservationist. He was a driving force in preserving Wilmington's Academy of Medicine and the Old Town Hall. Sharp had deep involvement in his alma mater, the University of Delaware. Its handsome campus, buildings and landscaping, are significantly a result of Sharp's efforts.

Reputedly, Sharp's Gibraltar had significant influence on his du Pont relatives as they built their grand country estates.

Ironically, his estate has fallen into neglect upon his son's (Hugh Rodney Sharp, Jr.) 1990 death. Heirs wanted to demolish the estate and erect condominiums but were stopped by efforts initiated by a descendent of the original Brinckle family.

The abandoned mansion began to leak and fall apart. The roof was repaired to prevent further deterioration. The garden went untended. (It had once required the care of seventeen gardeners.)

In 1997, Preservation Delaware took control of the grounds. In 2000, it opened the gardens (maintained at a minimum) to the public.

Wilmington police train their dogs on the grounds and in the old mansion.

In its derelict state, Gibraltar is still a marvel, arguably more fascinating and evocative because of its continuing deterioration and its questionable future. For now, it invites visitors to wander the garden without restrictions, to imagine what was, what might be, or simply enjoy the reflecting pool and 37 stony-muses selected by the Sharp family.

Though only a remnant of what once was, the gardenscape is still stunning.

Gibraltar is located at 1405 Greenhill Avenue, Wilmington.

WILLIAM PENN'S QUAKER LEGACY

32 - WILLIAM PENN

LONG AFTER HE ESTABLISHED HIS colony of Pennsylvania, William Penn's (1664-1718) legacy continues to influence the region Around the Delaware Arc.

Raised during the Puritan Era of Cromwell, his parents practiced the state Anglican religion. His family was exiled to Ireland by Cromwell, where the young Penn was introduced to the religious group known as the Quakers (The Religious Society of Friends).

Penn studied at Oxford. He continued to be attracted to the teachings and practices of The Religious Society of Friends (founded c. 1650), who were persecuted as dissenters after the Restoration. Penn converted to the Quaker way at age twenty-two (1686). His father did not approve, banishing his son and threatening to withhold his inheritance.

Penn fell under the influence and company of the radical Quaker leader George Fox.

Under Fox, Penn also became a leader of what continued to be a troublesome sect for the Crown. He wrote a biography of Fox. He set up demonstrations that challenged Crown law. He traveled to Germany and Holland to promote the Quaker way. He was jailed for his activities. Yet, in the process, he earned his father's admiration for his integrity, courage, and commitment to conscience. The Admiral decided not to disinherit his son.

Penn tried to persuade King Charles and James, Duke of York (the King's brother) that Britain would be more peaceful if the Quakers had a place to emigrate to. Thus, in 1681, Charles II, ostensibly to settle a debt owed to his deceased admiral father, made Penn the famous grant southeast of the Delaware River, west of New Jersey, and north of Maryland.

Penn had a sure sense of the colony he wanted to create. While still in England, he wrote a Frame of Government, that institutionalized his strong ideals, including religious toleration to all Christian groups and which included certain personal rights.

He planned Philadelphia as a "greene country towne" and expected the colony he would establish to be occupied along those lines. Among his designs was a basic home (surrounded by an acre of land) that became known as the Penn Plan house, which did serve as a model. (However, his tolerance and recruitment of persecuted German sects led not to such rural towns, but to prosperous farms that characterized Chester and Delaware Counties in particular).

Fellow Quakers who followed his lead established a culture of independence, peace, and justice. Penn provided an admirable example by fair (especially in regards to his times) dealings with the Lenni Lenape who inhabited the lands he and his heirs sold.

Penn's control was never absolute and an early Quaker governmental hegemony faced many challenges, particularly after Penn's death in 1718. His natural heir, his oldest son, was dissolute, so Penn disinherited him. Penn's wife and other three sons had practical control of the lands left.

Penn's desire for an ocean port to secure his holdings, led him to persuade James, Duke of York to cede to Penn the so-called Three Lower Counties (1683) that James held by squatter's sovereignty.

Penn's later years were troubled. He nearly lost the colony of Pennsylvania to the machinations of an unscrupulous manager. Embroiled in a host of legal issues, Penn spent time in debtors' prison. He died penniless.

That his statue atop Philadelphia's city hall, for decades the highest point in the city, still overlooks the place he designed and infused with ideals true to the meaning of "City of Brotherly Love," is appropriate.

What Penn called his "Holy Experiment," though only partially realized, was more than just an extraordinary religious intuition—the spiritual inner light of the Divine translated through Penn's practical imagination. It had, and continues to have, effect through a myriad of enduring attitudes and a few existing forms.

33 - WILLIAM PENN'S HOLY EXPERIMENT

William Penn had a particular religion (The Religious Society of Friends or Quakers) and from that religion came an expansive vision for the 40,000-acre grant west of the Delaware River, he received from Charles II in 1681. Penn declared, "It is a clear and just thing, and my God that has given it to me through many difficulties, will, I believe, bless and make it the seed of a nation."

In a letter to James Harrison, Penn wrote, "For my Country, I eyed the Lord in the obtaining of it, and more was I drawn inward to look to Him and to owe it to His Hand and Power than to any other, way. I have so obtained it, and desire that I may not be unworthy of His Love, but do that which may answer His kind Providence, and serve His Truth and People; that an Example may be set up to the nations; there may be room there, though not here, for such a 'Holy Experiment.'"

The main features of Penn's Holy Experiment were religious liberty and equality unrivaled any other place in the world. From a contemporary perspective, Penn promoted democracy, religious freedom, and social justice in dealing with the Native Peoples and with neighboring colonies, no standing militia, and the forgoing of oaths.

Penn deliberately did not make Pennsylvania an exclusive Quaker province. Penn advertised his vast lands for sale and religious freedom to a number of dissenting and often persecuted groups: fellow Quakers in England, Wales, and Ireland; French Huguenots; German Pietists and other Reformed sects at odds with Lutheran or Catholic authorities.

Penn also sought to forge treaties with the Native Peoples, compensating them for the lands he had been granted by royal decree. Through the mid-eighteenth century, the Commonwealth and the Native Peoples were relatively free from armed conflict.

Penn died in 1718. His sons who inherited his holdings were less faithful to his vision with the Lenni Lenape; indeed, they proved treacherous. The government of Pennsylvania remained Quaker controlled through 1756.

Though hard to measure, the influence of Penn's Holy Experiment had remarkable effect that many connect to core founding principles of the American Republic including Life, Liberty, and the Pursuit of Happiness.

The vision of the Holy Experiment is symbolically represented in the "Peaceable Kingdom" images of the Quaker artist Edward Hicks, painted in the first half of the nineteenth century, particularly the renderings that portray Penn negotiating the "Great Treaty" with the Lenni Lenape in the background and familiar peaceable animals in the foreground.

Surviving Friends Meeting Houses scattered throughout the area Around the Delaware Arc remind and remember William Penn's remarkable Holy Experiment.

34 - QUAKERS

WILLIAM PENN, THE PROPRIETOR OF a massive 1681 land grant from Charles II, was an important English Quaker. He founded his colony west of the Delaware and north of Calvert Maryland as a haven for Quakers from religious persecution in Britain and on the Continent. Pennsylvania's government remained under the control of Quakers through 1756.

The founding of The Religious Society of Friends (the sect's formal name) began during the yeasty ferment of the Cromwellian Revolution, circa 1650. This dissenting sect was organized in 1668. Its leading light George Fox mentored William Penn. Penn had been converted from his natal Anglicanism in 1686 at age twenty-two. Penn was instrumental in setting Quaker principles into a pamphlet, "Truth Exalted," which also was critical in pointing out the egregious beliefs of other forms of Christianity. For example, Penn labeled the Roman church "The Whore of Babylon."

The Quaker moniker was an outside judgment regarding the fervor that swept over the early adherents. The name of The Religious Society of Friends referenced a verse from the Gospel of John: "You are my friends if you do whatever I command."

The essence of Quaker practice was the doctrine of "inner light" that contended God speaks to each individual, directly and without mediation. Conscience predicates ethical behavior. Quakers eschewed traditional church forms including structured worship and the preaching of clergy. They called their houses of worship Meeting Houses, attending meetings not services. The Bible, while a revered source, was secondary to the authority of personal revelation. There tended to be a downplaying, if not rejection of certain orthodox Christian doctrines: the Trinity, heaven and hell, and original sin. Quakers were against oath-taking. Personal belief mattered less than the life-lived. The Kingdom of God was earthly, and it was the duty of Quakers to work for its realization. Though the Kingdom of God was within, it should be made manifest in society.

Quakers favored plain speech (*thou* and *thee*) and advocated plain dress. The Quakers generally practiced pacifism and were anti-military; yet they also engaged, often to great profit, in enterprise and industry. Though not originally abolitionist, Pennsylvania Quakers increasingly became anti-slavery in the 1740-1750s and onward. Women had a remarkable degree of participation in their Society's life. Straddling the Mason Dixon Line, Quakers became conductors and station masters of the Underground Railroad that assisted fugitive slaves reach freedom.

Many of the Quaker ways practiced by Penn and the early Quaker settlers were magnified in a schism between the Hicksites and the Orthodox (c. 1825); each group claiming to be the true descendant of George Fox's founding principles. It now is obvious that the Orthodox were infusing certain Evangelical values of the Second Great Awakening into their worship and organization; and the Hicksites rejected these practices. In the region Around the Delaware Arc, the Hicksites prevailed.

Arguably, the most influential Quaker values were religious toleration and fairness, especially toward the native people, the Lenni Lenape.

35 - QUAKER MEETING HOUSES

WILLIAM PENN WAS A MEMBER of the Society of Friends. He spoke of Pennsylvania as a "Holy Experiment." Many of early Pennsylvania colonists were British, Welsh, and Irish Quakers. The eighteenth century culture of Pennsylvania was infused with Quaker values.

Quakers worshipped in simple, small structures called meeting houses, often with a graveyard to one side and a shelter/shed for horses on the other. The grave markers also reflected simplicity, even humility–low stones inscribed with name and birth and death dates.

Around the Delaware Arc, a number of these meeting houses survive and many still function, invoking a living heritage of simplicity and peace intentions.

One of the earliest, Chichester Meeting, in Boothwyn, Pennsylvania (611 Meetinghouse Road) dates from 1769, erected after a 1688 building burned down. It is a fieldstone structure with a typical interior: two sections of pews divided into female and male sides by a partition with sliding windows, a wood stove in the center, and no ornamentation or symbolism. Its doors have bullet holes believed to have been fired by foragers roaming the countryside following the 1776 Battle of the Brandywine.

The famous African American artist of the first half of the twentieth century Horace Pippin, in several paintings, memorably rendered his unique vision of the Birmingham Meeting House, a few miles south of West Chester, Pennsylvania (1245 Birmingham Road, West Chester.) The Birmingham Meeting was in the thick of the Battle of Brandywine, serving as a hospital for both the Colonials and the British at different times during the battle. Colonials, British, and Hessian troops are buried in the adjacent cemetery.

The brick Centre Friends Meeting House, just south of the Delaware Arc in Centreville (Centre Meeting Road and Adams Dam Road) has a particularly beautiful setting. Centreville Friends first worshipped in a log building built in 1711. It was replaced in 1796 by the current structure with recent improvements updated.

Visitors are welcome to participate in the unprogrammed worship of the contemporary Friends who maintain these buildings and continue the founding religion of William Penn.

The Penn Plan House, the Pennsylvania Bay Barn, the Quaker Meeting House are three distinctive building forms of the region Around the Delaware Arc.

36 - PENN PLAN HOUSE

WILLIAM PENN PLANNED THE CITY of Philadelphia, centered on a 1,200 acre plot that was laid out in a rectangular grid. Orderly spaced, individual lots, an acre or half acre in size were large enough to provide room for discrete outdoor space to accommodate gardens. In Penn's plan, there was a large square centering four quadrants. Lettered and numbered streets ran perpendicular to each other. Broader streets served the purposes of commerce and transportation. The four quadrants of the original 1,200-acre plot had open, public green-space. Currently these are known as Rittenhouse, Franklin, Logan, and Washington Squares. Penn intended that his city to be framed as a "greene Country Towne."

Penn proposed a style of house for this country-like town he envisioned for Philadelphia and throughout his colony.

The Penn or Quaker Plan House (through 1800), with three rooms on the first floor, had a common room that ran from front to back with a large fireplace for cooking. A stairway rose to the second floor. There were also built-in cabinets. An interior wall separated the larger entrance room from two smaller rooms. The smaller rooms each had a single window, and perhaps a small fireplace. These smaller rooms might have served as bedroom, sitting room, or office. A second floor had additional sleeping rooms. The larger room was about the same size as the two smaller rooms combined. Its entry door was off- center relative to the front of the house and the large chimney was also to that side.

These houses were to be constructed of field or quarried stone, brick, log and/or wood sheathed in clapboard or stucco.

In 1684, advertising for colonists to come to Pennsylvania, Penn called his design a "beginner's house," because they were relatively small. Over time, many surviving Penn Plan houses in Chester and Delaware Counties acquired an addition or additions that generally strolled across the landscape with considerable grace.

A surviving, solitary Penn Plan house or one that has organically grown from fashion or necessity over time, particularly when constructed from multi-hued fieldstone, is one of the distinctive and compelling signatures of the region Around the Delaware Arc. It harkens to founding Quaker principles: simplicity, utility, domesticity, and industry.

37 - *WESTTOWN SCHOOL*

Q UAKERS LOST CONTROL OF THE
Pennsylvania state government in 1756.

During the Revolutionary War, with patriotism running high and war raging in Pennsylvania, traditional Quaker pacifism met a hostile culture. Vilified by some as traitors, Philadelphia Quakers felt their influence, indeed their way of life threatened as they declined economically and socially, as well as politically. They worried about the fate of their children. Would their children retain traditional Quaker values?

To answer the question of the moral development as well as general education of their children, Quakers planned carefully for a boarding school beyond the influences of the city that would afford their children an appropriate education. They chose a site of 600 acres some 25 miles west of Philadelphia in

Chester County. Forty students arrived in May 1799 at Westtown, Chester County. A score of boys and girls were added to the campus each month until there was a critical core of one hundred students of each gender in residence.

At first, the Westtown Friends School required plain dress and speech, including the use of *thee* and *thou*. Modesty and piety were part of the day's teaching that occurred from six o'clock in the morning through bedtime, with silence during meals and at night. Usefulness was a primary virtue. A family-like environment was cultured in the separate male and female dormitories. In 1833, formal studies in Quaker ways, including testimonies, became part of the curricula.

The land provided clay for the bricks of an impressive building and other out buildings. A campus farm provided much of the school's food.

The campus and region's Piedmont landscape inspired and provided recreation. Bobsledding down steep hills beyond the dormitory was a regular winter sport. A Westtown graduate, inventor Samuel L. Allen had students test his version of a sled with runners that could be directed by turning the front. The prototype they tried became the famous Flexible Flyer sled, patented in 1889.

After the Civil War, starting with skating on the school's 12 acre pond, classes and activities became increasingly coeducational, until in 1881 boys and girls were eating together. At the same time, the curricula and school terms were modernized.

A great main building of rich red brick was completed in 1888, giving the campus an impressive hub that creates the school's solid and distinctive look, harkening to a rich heritage and remembering the landscape.

N.C. Wyeth was a friend of the school. Commissioned to create art for the school, he settled on a huge painting, much like a book illustration, called "The Giant" (1923). In the painting, children play along the sea's edge and towering clouds (and the children's collective imagination) give shape to the giant's form. The painting remains on a dining room wall.

Westtown School continues to educate a diversity of students (some 650) in Quaker-rich studies and activities. It strives to maintain a practicing Quaker core in its upper grades. Boarding is required for junior and seniors.

The main entrance of the campus is located at 975 Westtown Road, West Chester, Pennsylvania.

38 - LONGWOOD PROGRESSIVE FRIENDS

LONGWOOD GARDENS' WEBSITE HAS A page dedicated to the Quaker heritage of the area, mentioning that the information center just outside the main gate is the former Longwood Progressive Friends Meeting House, built in 1855. When the Meeting disbanded in 1940, Pierre S. du Pont bought the building.

This building is now a convenient way of visiting a nineteenth century Quaker Meeting House.

Its museum-like qualities, however, don't begin to convey the once radical nature of this particular place, its involvement in the antebellum anti-slavery agitation, internal conflicts among the Society of Friends, and a continual involvement in the most radical aspects of the American Experience throughout the Meeting's nine decades.

In the 1850s, within ten miles of Longwood were some ten other Meetings. Chester County Quakers, particularly in this contained area, had leaned toward the abolition of slavery throughout the first half of the nineteenth century. The Kennett, Pennsylvania area north of the Delaware Arc was a major route of the Underground Railroad, for fugitives escaping north through Delaware to Wilmington—and then this final leg to free soil. Local Quakers received the fugitives from Wilmington and sent them on their way to Philadelphia. Longwood supposedly got its name from a final, long stretch of woods through which the fugitives passed.

In the decade before the Civil War, the Society of Friends contended among themselves about how to oppose slavery, whether by personal witness or public defiance.

Should their actions be apart from the world or of the world? (A few local Quakers were so scrupulous that they grew their own cotton, so as not to wear slave cotton.)

A radical Hicksite contingent of Quakers, who formed the Kennett Meeting, chose the vocally activist route. In 1853, they organized as the Progressive Friends Meeting of Longwood, Pennsylvania. When they dedicated their own building two years later, the Meeting proclaimed it received "all who regard mankind as one Brotherhood, and who acknowledge the duty of showing their faith in God, not by assenting to the lifeless propositions of a man-made creed, but by lives of personal purity and a hearty devoting to the welfare of their fellow men.

"Slavery, Intemperance, War, Capital Punishment, the denial of the Equal Rights of Woman, Oppression in all forms, Ignorance, Superstition, Priestcraft and Ecclesiastical Domination—these, and all such as these, are the evils and sins, which they feel constrained to assail by every rightful and legitimate weapon; while they seek to promote every virtue and to foster those principles of justice, mercy and love, which alone can secure the peace, progress and happiness of all the children of God."

These Progressive Friends were dedicated not to a single reform, but to a "sisterhood of reforms."

The controversial and radical Unitarian minister Theodore Parker spoke at the building's dedication in 1855. When the society closed its doors in 1940, the leading black civil rights leader A. Philip Randolph, the President of the Brotherhood of Sleeping Car Porters, spoke.

Between 1855 and 1940, despite a relatively remote, rural location along the Baltimore Pike (Route 1), the Longwood Meeting attracted an array of nationally important reformers to its programs. Lucretia Mott, William Lloyd Garrison, Sojourner Truth, Anna Howard Shaw, W.E.B. DuBois, Norman Thomas, and Roger Baldwin begin the list.

39 - PEACEABLE KINGDOM

THE MEANING OF WILLIAM PENN'S "Holy Experiment" found visible expression in a series of paintings by Quaker minister and painter Edward Hicks (1780-1849). The notion of a "Peaceable Kingdom" took biblical inspiration from the Old Testament Book of Isaiah: "The wolf shall also dwell with the lamb, and the leopard shall lie down with the kid; and the calf and the young lion and the fatling together; and a little child shall lead them."

Over a lifetime, Hicks' sixtysome paintings on this theme evolved. His later paintings not only depicted animals and a tender child in harmony, they included in the background, William Penn signing the "Great Treaty" with a Lenni Lenape chief. In the early Pennsylvania experience, Penn was deliberate in treating the Native Americans of his colony with remarkable respect, especially when compared to the parallel New England Puritan experience. Hicks emphasized Penn's integrity in signing treaties and the prevailing peace those treaties had established.

Hicks took the side of an older cousin in the controversy (c.1827) among Quakers regarding so-called original Quaker tenets or a newer version promoted by Elias Hicks. Hicksites emphasized the inner light, freedom, and leaned toward the abolition of slavery. (The Hicksites were actually resisting the innovations of evangelical enthusiasms associated with the Second Great Awakening that had crept into Quaker practice.)

Certain art historians read the Hicksite controversy into Edward Hicks' series of paintings portraying a Peaceable Kingdom. Hicks' famous images, however, continued to convey core Quaker values of Penn's Holy Experiment.

Quakers prevailed in Pennsylvania government through 1756. After the American Revolution, Quaker values in Pennsylvania were gradually displaced by values of the American Republic—values forged in revolution and annealed by war.

SINGLE TAX AND ARTS AND CRAFTS

40 – ARDEN

UTOPIA LITERALLY MEANS NOWHERE, BUT one of the most successful of all American utopian communities Arden, Delaware, has been somewhere since 1900. That somewhere is in northeastern New Castle County within the Delaware Arc.

The turn of the century was a fertile time of social and economic reform in reaction to Gilded Age excesses and sterile industrializations. British artist, designer, and social reformer, William Morris, associated with the Arts and Crafts Movement, inspired a generation of kindred spirits, including two Philadelphians: sculptor Frank Stephens and architect William Lightfoot Price.

Stephens and Price also advocated the radical economics of Henry George, a fellow Philadelphian they both personally knew. George's *Progress and Poverty* (1879) proposed a single land tax, maintaining that individuals should keep the profit of their labor, whereas the land–Nature's inherent resources–was held in common by all. He proposed that a single land tax would reduce economic inequalities while encouraging production.

Stephens and Price had joined other Georgites in a quixotic political campaign in 1895-96 for Single Taxers to win control of the small state of Delaware. The campaign quickly became the brunt of jokes. Georgites, including Stephens, were arrested for illegal demonstrations. Garnering scant enthusiasm from Delawareans, the campaign failed. But these two Georgites were not dissuaded.

Stephens and Price, with the financial support of soap manufacturer Joseph Fels, in 1900, purchased a 162 acre farm at Grubb's Corner, Delaware to establish a Single Tax community seasoned by the Arts and Crafts philosophy of William Morris.

Architect Price laid out the old farm to blend community and Nature, following the theory of *Garden Cities of Tomorrow* by another British visionary Ebenezer Howard. (Half of the original woods on this tract continue to be preserved.) Throughout its first decade, Arden was a weekend retreat and summer tent community. It gradually attracted leaseholders who built primitive cottages or cabins. By 1909, Arden claimed 50 permanent residents.

Upton Sinclair was an early resident. During his tenure as a University of Pennsylvania economics professor, Scott Nearing lived next to Sinclair. He later characterized his Arden sojourn as "the good life in miniature." A passer-through, the so called "Vagabond Poet" Harry Kemp, described the Arden he experienced in 1911 as consisting of "Single Taxers, Anarchists, Socialists, Communists—folk of every shade of radical opinion... who here strove to escape the galling mockeries of civilisation and win back again to pastoral simplicity."

Stephens posted a sign that became an Arden motto: "You are welcome hither" (a line from King Lear, echoing the Shakespearean origin of the name *Arden*.) Until his death (1953) Stephens was the "Patro" (Esperanto for *father*) of Arden who kept the founding spirit vital.

Through the years, Ardenites have had the reputation of being creative, artsy persons, who sought to practice tolerance with one another, fostering individualism and promoting community.

Property is leased, not owned, for ninety-nine years. In the tradition of its Single Taxers, residents are taxed on the value of their land, not on their improvements.

Arden's success was replicated in adjacent tracts became that became Ardentown (1922) and Ardencroft (1950). Together the three remarkable communities are known as the Ardens.

Harvey Road east of Marsh Road runs through the center of the three Ardens.

41 - ARDEN AND BLUE LAWS

IN ITS EARLY YEARS, THE utopian Arden colony, on principle, upheld freedom of speech. Many Ardenites were known as "confabulators," prominent for their public pronouncements from a radical-progressive point of view.

One confabulator proved a problem, an anarchist shoemaker named George Brown who frequently addressed the community when it gathered at meetings in the Guild Hall or the open-air theater. Many of his remarks were sexually salacious and tested the limits of Arden's notion of freedom of speech. The community argued about what, if anything, should be done about Brown. (Will Price suggested having him arrested for disturbing the peace.) After testing a couple of more benign strategies, founder and "Patra" Frank Stephens had Brown arrested.

Frank Stephens

Brown paid a fine, held his tongue, but plotted against his accusers.

Delaware had "blue laws," antique statutes that proscribed behavior on Sunday. One of the "blue laws" ambiguously prohibited gaming on

Sunday. (Did the ordinance refer to gambling or to the playing of sport?)

Arden had no police. The citizens preferred it that way. Anarchist Brown got his vengeance when he requested a Wilmington constable issue warrants for all "John Does" of Arden who would be playing baseball or tennis on a particular 1911 summer Sunday. Since he received two dollars per arrest, the constable agreeably arrested 11 Ardenites (including tennis-playing Upton Sinclair) and escorted them to Wilmington, where they were fined.

The Ardenites argued that they were being singled out, since members of the du Pont family were playing golf on that same Sunday with a judge at a Wilmington course. Rather than pay fines, the Arden 11 chose to serve their time (a day) in the workhouse. Before their incarceration, they enjoyed ice cream cones from a local parlor.

Playing off his muckraking reputation, Sinclair wrote a poem deploring conditions of the workhouse. A resident remembered, "The incident was closed by the Ardenites informing the authorities at Wilmington that if there was any more interference with 'worldly amusement' at Arden they would swear warrants in Wilmington for the du Ponts, Judge Grey and other residents for playing golf." The controversy then highlighted social class and political status.

The incident earned Arden an entire page in the New York Times, a somewhat tongue-in-cheek article accompanied by seven photos, including a prominent photo of Sinclair wielding a tennis racket.

This widely publicized affair further forged Arden's reputation as quirky and worthy of mockery.

42 - UPTON SINCLAIR

AT THE INVITATION OF FRANK Stephens, Upton Sinclair became an Arden resident in 1910. His 1906 expose of the Chicago meat packing industry, the novel *The Jungle*, made him one of the best-known progressives of the first decade of the twentieth century.

Sinclair had a utopian bent. In 1906, he established an experimental community, Helicon Home Colony in Englewood, New Jersey with proceeds from his novel *The Jungle*. Sinclair disavowed that he intended to create a socialist community, but demurred that it had socialist features. When the building burned down in 1907, the community disbanded.

Sinclair next lived in a Single Tax community in Fair Hope, Alabama before settling in Arden, becoming its most famous resident.

In 1910, with wife Meta Fuller and young son David, Sinclair was living in a tent on the common, adjacent to Scott Nearing's cabin, which Sinclair used as a writing studio when Nearing was teaching economics at the Wharton School. It was in Nearing's cabin that Sinclair caught Meta *in flagrante delicto* with the "Hobo Poet" Harry Kemp, whom Sinclair had invited to Arden in 1911.

Meta and Harry fled Arden. This initiated a much-publicized divorce, including Sinclair's own detailed account. Ironically, Sinclair had been working on a book, another novel, *Love's Pilgrimage*. (The dedication read: "To those who throughout the world are fighting for the emancipation of the world, I dedicate this woman's book.")

Sinclair, with other Ardenites, in 1911 was arrested for violating a Delaware "blue law," regarding gaming (did the statute mean playing games or gambling?) on Sunday. This event garnered national publicity for a community already looked upon with suspicion for its population of left leaning radicals and quirky personalities.

Though only briefly a resident of Arden, Sinclair left an enduring impression on one of the successful/enduring American utopian communities. The house he built before leaving was aptly named "Jungalow."

A year and a half after arriving in Arden, Sinclair moved to California, remarried, and ran a spirited campaign 1934 for Governor.

43 - UPTON, HARRY, AND META

UPON THE INVITATION OF ARDEN'S co-founder Frank Stephens, Upton Sinclair brought his wife Meta (married in 1902) and ten year old son David with him to the Single Tax Community of Arden, Delaware in the winter of 1910. They lived in a tent adjacent to Scott Nearing's weekend and summer cabin. Though their stay was brief, the Sinclairs focused national attention of this utopian community.

In the summer of 1911, Sinclair and ten other Ardenites gained national attention for "gaming" on Sunday, thereby violating the Sunday "blue laws." They were arrested, found guilty, and spent eighteen hours in the workhouse. This amusing episode was immortalized in a poem Sinclair tossed off while incarcerated: "The Menagerie" collected in *The Cry for Justice.*

Sinclair invited Harry Kemp, whom he had met at the University of Kansas, to join him in the Single Tax community of Arden. Kemp was known as the "hobo" or the "vagabond" poet with a favorable national reputation. Kemp arrived in Arden as the gaming-on-Sunday controversy was about to begin.

Sinclair had written about free love and marriage throughout his career. There is evidence that Sinclair and Meta each had at least one affair in their decade long marriage. He described the novel published during his brief Arden sojourn *Love's Pilgrimage* (1911) as "a novel about modern marriage that would show the possibility of a couple's agreeing to part, and still remaining friends."

Soon after Harry arrived in Arden, July 1911, Meta and Harry fell in love. Sinclair found them in Nearing's cabin engaged in sexual activity. Harry and Meta then "ran away," publicly enjoying, perhaps flaunting their relationship in New York City. Sinclair hired a detective to track them down. Sinclair began divorce proceedings in late August. In the interim, the three held a curious joint press conference, each explaining their sense of what love meant.

Later, Meta claimed that Sinclair could not sexually satisfy her. She characterized him as, "conservative by instinct and nature and radical merely by choice." She further added that she was only following Upton's advice regarding a woman's independence and self-fulfillment.

Sinclair appeared both the wounded husband and hypocrite philosopher. Unable to secure a New York divorce, he travelled to the Netherlands and divorced Meta there in 1912.

In a brief couple of years of residency, Upton Sinclair shone a light on Arden that the larger world found a matter of considerable humor, even ridicule.

44 – MONOPOLY

WHAT'S THE MOST FAMOUS OF all board games? Arguably, *Monopoly*, a game that invokes greed, has topped the list since Parker Brothers introduced it in 1935.

Try to imagine its origin and evolution at the turn of the century among idealists living in the quixotic, upstart Single Tax community of Arden. A young Quaker woman born in Illinois, Elizabeth (Lizzie) Magie, grew up infused in Henry George's Single Tax theory. While living in Maryland she became an interested visitor to Arden, soon after its founding in 1900.

She devised a board game to illustrate George's economic philosophy, introducing it to the Arden residents who played it with enthusiasm. Shortly before she patented *The Landlord Game* in 1904, she said, "Let the children once see clearly the gross injustice of our present land system and when they grow up,

if they are allowed to develop naturally, the evil will soon be remedied."

by Elizabeth magie Phillips

Among the early Arden players of *The Landlord Game* was Scott Nearing, who from 1906-1915 taught economics at the University of Pennsylvania. Nearing and others in the Arden orbit made their own linen "boards" and gradually revised the rules. Nearing used the game in the classes he taught at Wharton.

Early players took pride in not owning a manufactured game. Actual game boards were not manufactured until 1906. Spread by word of mouth, *The Landlord Game* became known as *Monopoly Auction* and then simply *Monopoly* as its popularity grew. In 1934, a Philadelphian sold a version of *Monopoly* to Parker Brothers.

In 1935, Lizzie relinquished her rights to *The Landlord Game* to Parker Brothers for 500 dollars, upon the promise that the company would reissue it as she had envisioned it: a teaching aid for George's Single Tax theory. The company soon reneged on its promise; but by then, Parker Brothers owned exclusive rights to the game that had evolved into the most famous board game of all: Monopoly.

45 - SCOTT NEARING

THE FATHER OF THE TWENTIETH century back-to-the-land movement and an early voice for sustainability, Scott Nearing (1883-1983), spent ten years in the new single-tax community of Arden, Delaware. Nearing had graduated from the University of Pennsylvania in Philadelphia and would teach through 1915 at the Wharton School of Economics.

In 1908, a friend asked Nearing to go with him to Arden to help survey a lot the friend had just leased. Nearing liked what he saw of this utopian experiment in the region Around the Delaware Arc. On the spot, he leased a half acre plot for 13 dollars a year. It was the last remaining piece of land on the main common. Perhaps it had been left vacant because the waters of the common drained into it.

Nearing called his plot of weeds, brambles, and undergrowth "as unlikely a living place as anyone could imagine." On weekends and in the summer he cleared the land and built a small but livable cabin of wood and stone named Forest Lodge. He added a garden, and grew organic vegetables, including fine pole lima beans. During his Arden years, he became a vegetarian.

In later years he wrote that he "took produce to the Saturday town market, played Shylock, Cassius, and Romeo in the town theater productions, and attended all the town meetings at which 'the good and welfare of Arden' was discussed." Nearing found these community meetings to be stimulating arenas of argument and debate.

He noted that the community was soon populated by more socialists than single-taxers; the single-tax cause was generally waning. He helped refine a favorite community game Landlord, which would evolve over the next three decades into Monopoly. He used Landlord as a teaching game at Wharton. In 1908 Upton Sinclair, who gained notoriety through the muckraking novel *The Jungle*, lived next door in a tent. Sinclair lived in Nearing's cabin in the winter.

Living in Arden through 1915 significantly shaped Scott Nearing's radical evolution, particularly in his primary area of interest, economic distribution. He progressed from being a mild liberal (according to Upton Sinclair) to a socialist, to such a communist that he was kicked out of the Communist party. He went on to become an original, with his own philosophy and living of the good life in his later years.

He fondly remembered Arden as "the good life in miniature."

46 - ROSE VALLEY

NEAR MEDIA, PENNSYLVANIA IS A small turn of the century Arts and Crafts community, Rose Valley, the vision of architect and political reformer, William Lightfoot Price.

Price had joined with Frank Stephens in the founding of the Single Tax utopian community of Arden, Delaware, in 1900. He designed a landscape for Arden that left much of the original woods standing and offered common open space, with plots tucked discretely together for dwellings that promised solitude but also promoted community. He subsequently designed a few significant Arden buildings.

Price never lived in Arden as did Stephens. Instead, Price purchased 80 acres at Rose Valley, where he more fully exercised his architectural vision. The landscape is more deeply sculpted at Rose Valley than at Arden.

There were standing buildings that Price incorporated into his overall plan. When Price arrived there were a dozen small cottages, two mills, and a celebrated stone home called the Bishop White House.

Price inspired an Arts and Crafts community cast in the philosophy of the English visionary William Morris: the form of a building should suit those who lived in and used those buildings—a marriage of purpose, place, and material.

The buildings of Rose Valley have a harmony of materials (stone and stucco sometime set with decorative tile accents). Though they are all different, a similar appearance (many-paned windows, buttresses, overhangs, and red tile roofs) unifies them into a single aesthetic, both organic and romantic. A few are grand structures, others quite modest.

A former bobbin mill (1840) on the main road through Rose Valley became the acclaimed Hedgerow Theater (founded 1923). Price's impressive Thunderbird Lodge, a studio house crafted from a pre-existing stone bank barn, suited handsomely fulfilled the purposes of artist couple Alice and Charles Stevens.

Price's description of the evolution of Thunderbird Lodge indicates his architectural genius: "The old barn standing near the road was converted into first and second floor studios, the old timber roof being rebuilt for the upper studio, and large windows and fireplaces being built into the old walls. The house rambles off from the fireplace and off the studios and is connected to them by an octagonal stair hall. It is built in part of fieldstone so like that in the old barn that it is almost impossible to tell old work from new. The upper part is of warm gray plaster, and the roof of red tile. All of the detail is as simple and direct as possible, and the interior is finished in cypress stained to soft browns and grays and guilty of no finish other than wax or oil."

Another Price masterpiece, and perhaps the most important structure in Rose Valley, though easy to overlook, is the *House of the Democrat* (1912) on Price's Lane. Price had promoted the notion of a comfortable, attractive, and affordable home that provided the necessities, plus a little more. He'd written a book on the subject, a collection and expansion of his *Ladies Home Journal* articles: *Home Building and Furnishing: Being a Combined New Edition of Model Houses for Little Money (1903)*. Scholars consider the *House of the Democrat* to be one of the most important buildings of the American Arts and Crafts movement.

The founders of the Rose Valley Associations had lofty plans that were not fully realized or realized at all, such as gathering a core of craftsmen to handcraft furniture, pottery, and books or using the falling waters to generate electricity.

Rose Valley survives largely intact. A visit to Rose Valley and a visit of Arden, together tease out the intellectual ferment at the turn of the century: the quest for a life of accessible beauty and simple utility joined with economic reform and cooperative living. These remnant dreams enchant our modern sensibilities.

47 - *THE HOUSE OF THE DEMOCRAT*

WILLIAM LIGHTFOOT PRICE (1861-1916) WAS A Philadelphia-trained architect who had a hand in the founding of two important idealistic communities at the turn of the century: the single-tax community of Arden, Delaware (1900 with Frank Stephens) and the Arts and Crafts community of Rose Valley, Pennsylvania (1901). Price laid out Arden's landscape of lots, lanes, and commons and also designed a few surviving buildings. Rose Valley, though not a Single Tax community, remains as an important site of Price's architectural vision.

Price had a few important commissions that demonstrated his versatility. He designed a chateau-like residence (1894) for Philadelphia steel magnate Alan Wood, Jr. known as Woodmont. (In the latter half of the twentieth century, Father Divine bought the property.) Price also designed the fantastic Atlantic City Marlborough-Blenheim Hotel (built 1905, demolished 1979).

At the turn of the century, he was particularly interested in designing a small home for an emerging middle class. In 1895, he co-published his bungalow designs in *Home Building and Furnishings*, describing in detail a home for a nuclear family, without servants. He also published articles about such a house in important magazines of the era, such as *The Ladies Home Journal* and Gustav Stickley's *American Craftsman* magazine.

In the latter magazine, Price wrote: "The house of the democrat: shall be set in a place of greenery; it shall be far away from its next for privacy and not too far for neighborliness; it shall have a little space knit within a garden wall; flowers shall creep up to its warmth and flow, guided, but unrebuked, over wall and low-drooped eves. It shall neither be built in poverty and haste nor abandoned in prosperity; it shall grow as the family grows; it shall have rooms enough for the privacy of each and the fellowship of all.

"A democratic house should have spacious, low, wide-windowed rooms warmed by fireplaces in the winter and cooled by shadows in summer. Finally, a democratic house should be a place where 'art shall mean work and work shall mean art.'"

True to the Arts and Crafts Movement, the notion of an artful abode of grace, refinement, and simplicity along the lines of "The House Beautiful," and growing out of his own insights,

Price built an example of his ideal small house in Rose Valley (1912). He called it the "House of the Democrat."

Authorities consider this "House of the Democrat" one of the most important buildings of the American Arts and Crafts Movement.

In the region Around the Delaware Arc, there are striking similarities between William Penn's "starter home," known as a Penn Plan House (c. 1680) and Will Price's "House of the Democrat" (c. 1900).

"The House of the Democratic" is located on Price's Lane, Rose Valley.

48 - HEDGEROW THEATER

RICH WITH ITS OWN HISTORY, ensconced in Will Price's Arts and Crafts community of Rose Valley, is Hedgerow Theater—a building and a tradition.

Part of Price's initial purchase of 80 acres, the building along the creek on Rose Valley Road was originally a gristmill. Then it became a bobbin mill. In the early years, after Rose Valley's founding, the three story old mill provided a studio for artist Francis Day and later Alice Barber Stephens. One of the incorporators of the community Howard Fremont Stratton taught art classes in it. A relatively well-known potter, William Percival Jervis opened a studio in the former mill in 1904.

Early on, Price saw the building as a guild hall and community center. The artisans and artists were not particularly successful and the Artsman (Guild) Hall became the center that Price first imagined. The "Folk" as the residents referred to themselves used the building for theater, music, and other social activities.

In 1922, the New York actor and director Jasper Deeter fell in love with the building, community, and the culture of the arts that marked Rose Valley. He determined to create a new sort of theater community, dedicated not to the commercial, rather to the artistic. Deeter turned the old mill *cum* Guild Hall, into the home of a repertory company that extolled theater dedicated to "truth and beauty" as a way of life.

Deeter's vision of a rotating repertory theatre was realized from 1923-1955. It was lauded as America's most successful such company. It was a pioneer in the not-for-profit community theater movement. Among the theater's accomplishments was its racial integration of its resident, local, and visiting artists. Recently cited by the theater community as the "mother of all Philadelphia theaters," Hedgerow has had a contemporary revival under the direction of alumna Penelope Reed, who after 1990 has served as Producing Artistic Director.

Deeter's Hedgerow Theater foreshadowed the regional not-for-profit theatre movement, established a racially integrated company of artists, and established Hedgerow as a seminal theatre for similar theaters throughout the country.

In the 1930s, the repertory company had as many as 50 resident actors at one time. Among the company in the 1940s were future film stars Richard Basehart and Van Heflin. Today there are nine full time members of the company.

In 1985, the original building was nearly destroyed in an arson fire. Surviving features were saved. The restored building has larger indoor space and more amenities for actors and patrons than the original, while remembering the original mill structure, as modified by Rose Valley's founder Will Price.

The Hedgerow Theater is located in the heart of Rose Valley at 64 Rose Valley Road, Media.

WILMINGTON

49 - BRANDYWINE SUPERFINE FLOUR

THROUGHOUT THE EIGHTEENTH CENTURY, CHESTER County, Pennsylvania was America's most bountiful farming region. Wheat, among a variety of grains, was a leading product. To process the grain, modest gristmills appeared along the tumbling creeks, throughout the fall line of the Piedmont. The Conestoga wagon, it is surmised, was developed to supply the Piedmont mills with grist.

The Brandywine was a major creek of the region. After passing through Wilmington, it flowed into the Christiana River, which flowed to the Delaware and to the Atlantic Ocean. By mid-century, industrious Quaker millers had built gristmills and races to run the water wheels in the area now known as Brandywine Village, where the Creek enters the city. (Race Street in Wilmington remembers that heritage. On the south side of

the creek, the remains of a race can still be discerned.

It was a fortuitous union of circumstances: grain, especially wheat from Chester County, rapidly falling water to run the mills, and proximity to the Delaware River and beyond along the Atlantic Coast.

In the last decade of the eighteenth century, it was estimated that the Brandywine mills had the capacity to mill 500,000 bushels of wheat and corn, actually milling 300,000 bushels, with 50,000 bushels worthy of being called "superfine flour."

For much of the century after the mid-eighteenth century, Wilmington was America's primary flour manufacturer. Production gradually waned through the last half of the nineteenth century. The mills are gone with few reminders of their significance.

Brandywine Superfine Flour made Wilmington mills famous, even in Europe. Superfine Lane above Brandywine Mills Park remembers the union of varied assets: Piedmont soils; falling waters to power mill; human industriousness to grow, haul, and grind grain; and technologies such as Conestoga wagon and gristmills.

50 - BLACK POWDER

ÉLEUTHÈRE IRÉNÉE DU PONT DE NEMOURS (1771-1834) fled France with his father and brother, plus his brother's family, arriving at Rhode Island on January 1, 1800. Before their exile, the family had been embroiled in the French Revolution and its aftermath.

Irénée (also E.I.) was a chemist with a working knowledge of black powder. He had particular expertise in the manufacture of saltpeter (potassium nitrate) one of three components of black powder, having studied with the famed chemist Antoine Lavoisier.

The family, at least the father, had considered creating a model French émigré community named Pontania in America. Instead, Irénée established (1802) a powder mill on the banks of Delaware's Brandywine Creek, north of Wilmington, at Hagley. One of the features of the site was the willow trees that made a high-grade charcoal, a second component of black powder. The third ingredient, sulfur, could be transported by ship up the Delaware River to the nearby Christiana River, where wagons hauled it to the mill.

Black powder (with a few improvements from the original product) was the Du Pont Company's basic product through much of the nineteenth century, until other explosives (such as dynamite) took over the explosives marketplace. The Hagley Yards, along the Brandywine Creek north of Wilmington, once the world's largest manufacturer of black powder, operated through 1921.

Black powder proved recession proof thanks to wars, railroad construction, and westward expansion generally. The quality of the product recommended du Pont powder to the federal government. For example, du Pont provided forty per cent of the powder used by the Union army and navy during the Civil War. The Du Pont Company had such a hold on the manufacture of explosives, through an infamous Powder Trust, that in 1912 it lost a famous anti-trust judgment. Still, the United States requested the Du Pont Company continue to provide powder and explosives during World War I.

In fact, the du Pont interests provided upwards of 40% of the Allies' munitions. Revenues from the sale of powder and explosives soared from $25 million in 1914 to $319 million by 1918, totaling $1.245 billion during the war. In the 1930s, castigated as Merchants of Death and subject of a Congressional Hearing, the Du Pont Company was accused of $100 million in fraud and overcharges to the government during the world war.

The Hagley property (200 Hagley Road), open to the public, includes restored mills, a workers' community, and the ancestral home and gardens of the du Pont family.

51 - THOMAS GARRETT OF QUAKER HILL

FUGITIVE SLAVES ESCAPING NORTH THROUGH the Delmarva Peninsula found Quaker sympathizers throughout Delaware. In Wilmington, a Quaker merchant, Thomas Garrett (1789-1871) was a famous station master of the Underground Railroad, an informal network of abolitionists willing to break the law to shelter and assist fugitive slaves to freedom.

The famous Mason Dixon Line, the boundary between Pennsylvania and Maryland in the antebellum era, became the popular distinction between Free and Slave States. Delaware was a border state with a small population of slaves, mostly in southern Sussex County. It also had a large number of free blacks, reputedly the most relative to the total population of any state, particularly in Wilmington.

As a final stop on the Underground Railroad before ostensible freedom in Pennsylvania, Wilmington was something of a funnel that concentrated Delmarva Peninsula fugitives. It also attracted fugitive slave bounty hunters, adding danger for conductors, as well as for the runaways.

Garrett was born into a prosperous, landed Quaker family in Upper Darby. (The family home still exists in contemporary Drexel Hill, Delaware County.) His family assisted fugitive slaves.

As a youth, a female black servant was kidnapped by slave catchers. He was among those who intervened, which resulted in what he called a transcendent experience. A voice spoke to him, saying "help and defend this persecuted race." This incident set the course of his later activist life. In this regard, his choice to live in Wilmington with his family, circa 1822, seems deliberate to better assist fugitive slaves.

He lived on Quaker Hill, near the Wilmington Meeting House (401 North West Street). He established a hardware business. He became a famous station master and later reckoned that he helped 2,300 fugitives to freedom.

A series of legal wrangling resulted in a famous 1846 trial, when Garrett and a fellow activist were sued in Federal Court under the Fugitive Slave Act of 1793. The notorious Chief Justice of the Supreme Court Roger B. Taney presided over six trials, fining Garrett the considerable amount of $5,400. Garret told Taney, "Thou has left me without a dollar,...I say to thee and to all in this court room, that if anyone knows a fugitive who wants shelter...send him to Thomas Garrett and he will befriend him."

In 1870, in the wake of the 15th Amendment, affirming black Americans right to vote, Garrett was carried through Wilmington streets by black friends who called him "our Moses." Similarly, a year later upon his death, his coffin was passed from shoulder to shoulder by his black admirers to its interment on the grounds of the Wilmington Meeting House at 4th and West Streets on Quaker Hill.

The Meeting House still stands, though Garrett's House in the neighborhood has been razed.

In Wilmington, Garrett is associated with Harriet Tubman, co-conspirator in the Underground Railroad during two perilous decades before the Civil War. A peaceful park along the Christiana River at the Market Street Bridge remembers these courageous souls and the cause of human freedom they represented.

52 - HARRIET TUBMAN

HARRIET TUBMAN'S (1819-1913) EXTRAORDINARY LIFE HAS as its focus her role as a "conductor" on the Underground Railroad. As a conductor, she led some 300 fugitive slaves on perilous journeys up the Delmarva Peninsula (some 75 miles through Delaware) to Wilmington. At Wilmington, often with the assistance of "station master" Thomas Garrett, the fugitives would be secretly escorted into Pennsylvania and freedom. As an almost final stop, Wilmington was known as "Freeedomland."

A common route beyond Wilmington followed the old Kennett Pike to Longwood, where a concentration of Quaker abolitionists assisted fugitives seeking freedom. Even among themselves, Quakers argued about practicing civil disobedience in aiding fugitive slaves. A radical Hicksite contingent formed their own Meeting at Longwood near Kennett Square in 1854. The Longwood Quakers and allies received the fugitives and sent them to Philadelphia and other free locations.

Legend holds that the name Longwood came from a rank of trees through which the fugitives crossed into Pennsylvania. The Longwood Meeting disbanded in 1940; however, their meeting house survives as a visitor's information center along Route 1 behind the Kennett Square firehouse.

Since the Underground Railroad violated the law of the land and since bounty hunters sought information regarding routes of runaway slaves, there is scant documentation of the activities that reached a crescendo in the decade before 1865.

To remember this history, the Harriet Tubman Underground Railroad Byway (2012) through Delaware traces the route that Harriet Tubman likely followed with her small groups of fugitive slaves from Sandtown at the Maryland border to Wilmington's Quaker Hill.

The city has established a park below Quaker Hill along the Riverfront Park dedicated to the collaborators Harriet Tubman and Thomas Garrett. The Tubman-Garrett Park is near the Market Street Bridge, where it crosses the Christiana Bridge, a place where fleeing slaves concentrated, a dangerous point in the journey to freedom.

In 2012 a dramatic bronze statue "Unwavering Courage in the Pursuit of Freedom," depicting Harriett Tubman, representative fugitive slaves, and Thomas Garrett was unveiled at the Tubman-Garrett Park near the Market Street Bridge.

53 - RIVERFRONT WILMINGTON

IN 1988, THE CITY OF WILMINGTON, Delaware initiated an ambitious project to transform a decayed area along the Christiana River, south of the train station at the foot of the downtown. Envisioned as a mixed use of storefronts clustered together, museums, theaters, restaurants, riverwalk, baseball stadium, convention center and more, it is a cleverly unified designed. Cranes preserved from the Dravo Shipyard remember World War II industry at Dravo Plaza.

Forlorn but in good repair, the large cluster of shops currently sits mostly empty, but the other amenities and venues appear to be flourishing.

Just a little south of the shops, on the Christiana River is a unique urban wildlife preserve, Russell W. Peterson Wildlife Preserve with an adjoining educational center.

The setting begs a leisurely one and a third mile stroll from Tubman-Garrett Park at the Market Street Bridge to the Peterson Wildlife Preserve. Along the way, placard signs describe and illustrate Wilmington history, in aggregate, a quick but thorough treatment of the city's history from the arrival of the Swedes (1638) in the middle of the seventeenth century through today. The replica Swedish ship *Kalmar Nyckel*, an impressive tall ship from the colonial era, is often moored at Dravo Plaza.

There are plenty of benches and settings for sitting and enjoying the slowly flowing river and the distant city skyline. Toward the wildlife preserve, birds and animals appear. A few restaurants offer opportunities for outdoor or indoor food and drink. In season, a 29-passenger water taxi plies the river, picking up and dropping off passengers at five locations.

Of note are the museums: Delaware Sports Museum and Hall of Fame, The Delaware Museum of Contemporary Art, and Delaware Children's Museum.

The train station (1908), designed by an eminent nineteenth century Philadelphia architect, Frank Furness, forms a northern boundary to the Riverfront area. Recently, a 14 screen cinema began operation that promises more than the usual Hollywood fare: the likes of classic features, independent films, IMAX Documentaries, and other alternative content.

One of the advantages of the Riverfront Complex is ample and free parking, plus the visible patrols of bicycle-riding-security.

There are indications that the Riverfront's tourist appeal is growing.

As an entity, the Riverfront development is an example of contemporary urban redevelopment, designed not to suit the needs of nearby urban residents, but to return to the city arts, recreation, and entertainment gone from its former core. It is worth a visit on its own merits of urban planning, design, and execution.

54 - RUSSELL W. PETERSON WILDLIFE REFUGE

MANY OF THE PIEDMONT CREEKS of the region Around the Delaware Arc drain into the Christiana River as it approaches Wilmington, primarily Brandywine Creek and White Clay Creek. On a narrow band of coastal plain, the Christiana River meets the Delaware River. In Colonial days, this access to Atlantic Ocean trade, combined with mills at the Piedmont's nearby fall line to generate significant industry in flour milling, gunpowder making, and textile weaving and processing. (Today the Port of Wilmington is a major banana and fruit port.)

In the Riverfront Section of Wilmington, just south of the downtown area, are a number of attractions: large restaurants and small museums, a baseball stadium, indoor and outdoor concert venues, a section of mostly unoccupied storefronts, and a promenade for walking or biking along the river. Remnant structures of cranes from shipbuilding days hint at the area's former industrial days.

A little further south of this recently redeveloped area, accessed by a short, winding road for cars or by the riverwalk for pedestrians is one of the lesser known gems of the region's conservation and recreation areas, the 212 acre Russell W. Peterson Wildlife Preserve, one of a handful of such urban refuges in the nation. The grounds invite an easy boardwalk stroll through sprawling marsh and quiet contemplation at the river's edge. Plans include more restoration of the marsh and wetlands, including the river itself. More walking trails will access what is cited as one of the most important marshland refuges in the country.

The entrance to the refuge is attractively landscaped and well maintained. The refuge's multi-purpose building allows for an extended vista from the four story DuPont Environmental Education Center (2009) that rises above the preserve.

Russell W. Peterson (1916-2011) was one of Delaware's fascinating persons of the second half of the twentieth century. He was governor (1969-1972), scientist (a research chemist, he headed du Pont's research and development division), and activist (including prison reform). When governor, he removed the National Guard from Wilmington, who were occupying the city after the King Assassination riots. He was an avid birder. After his stint as governor, he headed the National Audubon Society. He was also an Ardenite, active in that quixotic village's affairs.

The address of the Peterson Refuge is 1400 Delmarva Lane, accessed by road south of the Shipyard Shops in Wilmington's Riverfront complex.

55 - DELAWARE ART MUSEUM

IF THE BRANDYWINE RIVER MUSEUM is a figurative shrine to the Wyeth family, the Delaware Art Museum is a literal shrine to the founder of the Brandywine School of Illustration, Howard Pyle, a Wilmington, Delaware native. The museum's origin dates from Pyle's unexpected death in 1912, when his widow sold a collection of a 100 of her husband works to the Wilmington Society of the Fine Arts, an organization that had sprung up to pay tribute to its famous native artist.

Through 1922, the WSFA held an annual exhibition of their Pyle works in conjunction with a juried show of illustrators. The WSFA next rented three rooms in the new Public Library as a more permanent venue. In 1931, the Society accepted the gift of Samuel Bancroft Jr.: 11 acres of land in northern Wilmington and his beloved collection of Pre-Raphaelite paintings. The WSFA raised $350,000 for a new building, which opened in 1938. The name was changed to the Delaware Art Center with the new building; and in 1972, the institution was renamed as the Delaware Art Museum. In 2005, a 30 million dollar, three year redesigns and expansion project was completed.

As it expanded through the years, the Museum has added to its core collections of Pyle and his fellow Brandywine School illustrators, as well as to Bancroft's significant gift of British Pre-Raphaelite canvasses. The museum has collected nineteenth and twentieth century art, including more than 5,000 pieces of John Sloan's work. It also has a representative collection of American illustrators through the years.

The Museum's library has materials relating to the original Pyle pieces and Bancroft's Pre-Raphaelite collection with a large deposit of Sloan related materials.

On a quiet, spacious city boulevard (2301 Kentmere Parkway, Wilmington), the Museum has space for a 9-acre sculpture garden, with a large labyrinth cunningly converted from a pre-existing water reservoir.

Despite the redesign and expansion, this relatively small museum continues to evoke the era and sensibilities of the early twentieth century. The dignified Rockford Park neighborhood is a fine setting for turn of the century book and magazine illustration now identified with Pyle's Brandywine School of Illustration.

The residential neighborhood, with wide streets and gracious homes, also reflects the tone of the "Golden Age of Illustration." The museum is located at 2301 Kentmere Parkway, Wilmington, Delaware.

Pyle's home and studio (which he built in an English Tudor style) is located not far from the museum on 1305 North Franklin Street, between Pennsylvania and Delaware Avenues.

56 - BIG AUGUST QUARTERLY

PETER SPENCER (1779–1843) WAS BORN A slave in Kent, Maryland. When his slave-master died, Spencer was freed. He moved to Wilmington, Delaware where he affiliated with the Asbury Methodist Church.

With fellow African American members, he was denied full participation in the life of the church. An extraordinary leader, Spencer led a group of 40 fellow African Americans that founded its own congregation, the Union Church of African Members. It was the first (1813) incorporated church denomination of, by, and for African Americans.

At first, Spencer's group did not intend to create their own denomination, just their own Methodist church. Their first service was held in a little grove between Lombard and Pine Streets above Fourth Street in Wilmington.

They continued to meet in a house at Fifth and French Streets. Then they acquired a lot at Ninth and French Streets, eventually building their own church. All of this took place in 1805.

Despite such remarkable accomplishments, this Spencer-led group found that the Methodist hierarchy would not grant them any rights in conducting their own church's business. Chafing at this injustice, they incorporated in 1813 and began what now known as African Union First Colored Methodist Protestant Church and Connection. They continued to meet at the Mother Church, Ninth and French Street through 1969, when urban renewal displaced them from their historic home.

This Church was also the site for the Big Quarterly Meeting (also known as the Big August Quarterly) a yearly gathering that looked to a Quaker model. The first Big Quarterly was held in 1814, a reunion and revival that grew into an annual festival that brought thousands of African Americans from the Delmarva Peninsula to Wilmington on the last weekend in August. Before the Civil War, it was common for masters to give their slaves a pass to attend, though scholars suggest that the Big Quarterly also contributed to the growth of the Underground Railroad: the Mother Church and Big Quarterly have been called a "gateway to freedom." The Big Quarterly has continued, yearly, since 1814, making it the longest continuing African American celebration in the country.

The Big Quarterly waned in the twentieth century; however, efforts in recent years have sought to renew earlier enthusiasms. The Tubman-Garrett Park on the Christiana River at Market Street is one of the venues for the events in August.

The relocated Mother African Union First Colored Methodist Protestant Church is located at 812 North Franklin Street.

57 – ROCKWOOD

J OSEPH SHIPLEY (1795-1867) WAS BORN INTO a Wilmington, Delaware Quaker milling family. He took his education at the Quaker boarding school, Westtown School east of West Chester in Chester County.

Rather than join the family company, Shipley first worked for a Philadelphia counting firm and then for an import and export business. Within four years (1819), he was representing the company in Liverpool, England. There, he also joined a merchant-banking firm (1825). He played a significant role in saving that firm from bankruptcy during the Panic of 1837 and was made a partner.

In 1846, Shipley rented a suburban villa outside of Liverpool, Wyncotte, designed by George Williams, a Victorian manor house with surrounding landscaped grounds, including an

English naturalistic style of garden. Shipley fell in love with the aesthetic and began to plan replicating it in his home city of Wilmington.

At the age of 50, he began to suffer from severe gout, the wealthy person's malady. A bachelor, he determined to retire close to family. In the middle of the nineteenth century, he toured his native Wilmington in search of suitable property.

He set his desires on the Brandywine Hundred farm of Levi Weldin. It had a view of the Delaware River, plus cliffs, a stream, and an impressive stand of chestnut trees. Shipley's nephew negotiated the purchase of parcels of land around the Weldin farm, and finally in 1851 acquired the key Weldin property. (Realizing Shipley's wealth, the farmer had been holding out for as much money as he could get.)

Shipley's nephew bought more surrounding land to complete a 382 acre estate that would be known as Rockwood. In 1851, Shipley returned to Wilmington with a few staff, horse and dog, household goods, and a flair for relatively refined design in an English country style.

Rockwood was Shipley's translation of the Victorian English Country Estate he had grown to love in England. George Williams designed the twenty-room Mansion after the fashion of Wyncotte. Williams further designed stables and carriage house, a lodge, and additions to the mansion. Shipley chose a simpler lodge design, though, using Baltimore architects, who also designed the gardener's cottage (1858).

Shipley's estate today is best-known as an early and well-conceived example of the Naturalistic Style of English landscape design (beginning c. 1730) with more modern touches of the picturesque, a reaction to the formal French and Italian styles with straight lines and topiary tamed landscape. The English garden utilized trees, curving walkways, and sweeping lawns, protected by ha-has. A ha-ha is a low, trenched wall on descending land that retards animals from the lawn, while providing the illusion of no barrier to an uphill observer. (An important element of the vista from Rockwood's extended back porch, looking toward the Delaware River, were sheep and cows grazing on descending pastures.)

It appears that Shipley, in collaboration with his imported English gardener, may have created much of his estate's landscape design. The Naturalistic Style of Rockwood made a favorable impression on American gardens; though in the final couple of decades of the nineteenth century, Arts and Crafts influences made a less fussy style more popular.

A few of Shipley-planted trees survive, including several spectacular specimens: a Weeping European Beech, an American Black Gum, a Chinese Gingko, and a clump of rhododendron.

Rockwood passed through the family until 1973 when the County of New Castle acquired it as a 72-acre park. The house, furnished with pieces true to the 1890s, has gone through restoration, as have other buildings. A picturesque conservatory awaits repair.

Rockwood's Gardenesque landscape is worthy of an imagination-evoking promenade with long vistas, curving paths, picturesque boulders, and trees and shrubs bordering the lawn. It remains a little patch of mid-nineteenth century, country England at the foothills of the Appalachian Piedmont north of the city of Wilmington.

Enter this New Castle County Park at 610 Shipley Rd, Wilmington.

ROUTE 13 CORRIDOR

58 - FOX POINT STATE PARK

PRESERVATION AND CONSERVATION HAVE RESULTED in considerable green space and/or public lands that characterize the region Around the Delaware Arc. A third and less common effort, remediation, takes problematic land and restores it.

An extraordinary example of remediation is Fox Point State Park in Delaware at Edgemoor, between Claymont and Wilmington, on the Delaware River. It is adjacent to a chemical plant operated by the Du Pont Company since 1935. The Du Pont Edgemoor facility produces titanium dioxide, an important component of paints and papers. (On this site was a Victorian mansion, Ellerslie, rented by F. Scott and Zelda Fitzgerald from 1927-1929, where he worked on *Tender Is the Night*. The house was used briefly by the Du Pont Company when the Edgemoor plant was built, but it was subsequently torn down.)

Though the setting gives it away, Fox Point was not named for the region's famous form of wealthy recreation and the wily animal of its pursuit. It was named for a dogged, early environmental activist S. Marston Fox. Beginning in 1958, Fox advocated that the Pennsylvania Railroad stop filling the riverbank with industrial waste and sewage sludge to create industrial land along its right of way. He also advocated the site be transformed into a riverside public park.

The four-mile strip of riverfront fell to public control in 1970s. After Fox's death in 1982, the Fox Point Civic Association continued to promote Fox's vision. In 1990 New Castle County turned the land over to the

State, beginning a complex remediation process, converting the first 15 acres of soil from toxic to safe via a "cap system."

After sand for drainage was applied, an impermeable layer of plastic was placed over the surface. This was covered with layers of sand, clean fill, and topsoil, suitable for the growth of plants and safe for general public use. These first 15 remediated acres were opened to the public on Earth Day 1995.

Phase II of the remediation process (completed on Earth Day 2009) similarly made safe 40 acres of toxic landfill to the north. The completed project of 55 acres of remediated riverfront has landscaping with native plants, paths, sitting places and overlooks, and state of the (environmental) art facilities, including self-composting outhouses.

The view up the river looks to Philadelphia. The downriver view includes the Delaware Memorial Bridge joining New Jersey with Delaware. The Delaware is a working river and ships pass Fox Point.

More than unique, this extraordinary former toxic dumpsite stretches for four miles along the river and includes 171 total acres. Juxtaposed to the Du Pont Company's Edgemoor (titanium dioxide) Plant, Fox Point Park invites the visitor to reflect upon the consequences of industrialization on the environment, the costs of remediation, and possible results.

Fox Point Park is located on Hay Road, Wilmington north of the Du Pont Edgemoor Plant.

59 - THE PATIO

One of the large financial personalities of the early twentieth century was John J. Raskob (1879-1950), whose career and influence was tied to the fortunes of the Du Pont Company. Pierre S. du Pont hired him in 1901 to be a personal secretary. By 1911, Raskob was an assistant treasurer of the Company. In 1918, he was vice president for finance of both the Du Pont Company and General Motors, in which the Du Pont Company had a heavy investment. (On Raskob's urging and Pierre S. du Pont's assent, the Company had acquired 43% of General Motor's stock.) During his General Motors tenure, Raskob invented consumer credit through General Motors Acceptance Corporation.

Raskob was a Democratic and Catholic, becoming chair of the Democratic National Convention. He backed Al Smith for president in 1928. Raskob's Claymont, Delaware estate, The Patio, hosted many strategy sessions for Smith's campaign.

Under pressure from Alfred P. Sloan, Raskob resigned from General Motors in 1928. With his mentor Pierre du Pont, Raskob made a large investment in the construction of the Empire State Building, circa 1930. He is often credited as its builder.

In 1910, Raskob moved his family (he and his wife Helena would have 13 children) from Wilmington to Claymont along the Delaware River to a relatively modest mansion on 48 acres known as Archmere. Raskob dreamed of a genuine manor house, more in line with those being built by the du Pont family, who were establishing their country manors in the Brandywine Valley.

Helena and he had fallen in love with the architecture of St. Augustine, Florida. The idea of a great open courtyard at the center of a square of rooms became possible through the new technology of a retractable skylight that suited a colder Mid-Atlantic climate.

From 1916 through 1918, what became known as "The Patio," was built in an Italian Renaissance style. The vast interior, guided by Raskob's eye for detail and made possible by his Du Pont and General Motors' riches, was opulent. In addition to the courtyard's Tiffany-like, retractable skylight, The Patio featured a marble fountain surrounded by statues of his 13 children.

The aspirations of The Patio are amply revealed in an account that Raskob offered in 1921, as he introduced readers to his Claymont estate in a book of family genealogy.

"Probably the first objects likely to attract the notice of visitor approaching 'Archmere' would be well-proportioned and beautiful iron gates at the entrance. But a visitor once inside the gates, and especially one who has traveled to Italy and visited Florence, would at once note the resemblance of the porte-cochere to the one which stands before the Pazzi Chapel, and would doubtless recall the story of the Prince of Pazzi rode backwards on a donkey from the Palestine to Florence, carrying a taper which had been lighted from the Holy Fire."

Claymont became increasingly industrial and proletariat. Raskob was spending less time in Wilmington.

In 1932, he sold The Patio estate to the Norbertine Order for 300,000 dollars. They established a Catholic boys' college preparatory school, Archmere Academy. Originally, classes were held in the Raskob mansion.

Archmere Academy, including the Raskob mansion, is located at 3600 Philadelphia Pike, Claymont.

60 - Marcus Hook

The Route 13 corridor through Delaware and Pennsylvania follows the path of the Delaware River through a post-industrial landscape. It is not a "designated scenic byway"–far from it. However, it offers an authentic (blue-collar) experience of the region Around the Delaware Arc with a crumbling vision of varied industries that sustained a string of communities. This region supported a steel plant and foundries, oil refineries, a Congoleum rug plant, shipyards, a helicopter plant, and more.

Marcus Hook, Delaware County, Pennsylvania north of the Delaware Arc, was long known for its main industry, a Sun Oil refinery. Following the discovery of the famous Spindeltop Oil Field in East Texas, the founder of Sun Oil, Joseph Newtown Pew, purchased 82 acres of the Lindenthorpe estate on the Delaware River to build a refinery to process Texas Crude.

The first tanker of oil arrived in 1902, and the site produced gasoline through 2011, when the plant was closed. Of significance, it was at the Marcus Hook refinery that the first catalytic cracker went into production, producing high-grade aviation fuel. The plant was essential to the war effort, providing 41 million gallons of petroleum to the Allies, the most of the entire oil industry.

The Marcus Hook refinery's 2012 closing with the loss of nearly 500 jobs, resonated throughout the one industry community, threatening the borough and local school's budgets as well.

In 2013 it appears that the refinery will reopen as a liquid natural gas processor and export terminal (ethane and propane), utilizing Marcellus Shale natural gas originating in Western Pennsylvania.

The tanks, cracking towers, and related paraphernalia of twentieth oil refining remain, reminding locals and visitors, too, of changes of post-industrial America and the costs of energy processing.

Further north on Route 13 is the abandoned (1970) plant of American Viscose, the site of the first synthetic fiber production in the United States (1910). It produced artificial silk, named *rayon* in the 1920s. At its height, it employed some 5,000 workers.

Across from the main building is Viscose Village, constructed from 1912-1915. It was a hybrid place (261 two-story homes, two boarding houses, and a store): a company town combined with a Garden City concept. It took inspiration from British factory towns utilizing an overall English Domestic Revival style. Its strong sense of community endures.

Arguably, the area's most famous son is Marcus Hook born baseball legend, Mickey Vernon (1918-2008). He is remembered by a life-size statue (2003) at a park named after him at Seventh and Market Streets in Marcus Hook. Vernon was a two time American League batting champion, who, playing for the lowly Washington Senators, was considered to be not just a quiet gentlemen, but one of the era's better players of Major League Baseball. There is also a Delaware County sports museum, the Mickey Vernon Sports Museum, located in the Granite Run Mall (1067 W Baltimore Pike, Media, Pennsylvania), with much Vernon-related material.

61 - *PENN'S UPLAND LANDING*

ON AUGUST 30, 1682, THE *WELCOME* BROUGHT William Penn from England to America. The ship was laden with a plenty of foods and the personal goods of a hundred some fellow passengers, mostly Quakers from Sussex. Along the way, smallpox broke out and thirty passengers and crewmembers died.

On October 26, the *Welcome* reached New Castle in the Three Lower Counties (now Delaware). Representatives of the Dutch, English, and Welsh settlers presented Penn with turf, twig, and a small metal bowl containing river water. (The contemporary New Castle historical district, with brick streets, restored homes and businesses, and several buildings of historic importance, honors Penn with a life-size statue in the midst of New Castle's common.)

The following morning, the ship sailed up the river and moored near the Swedish village of Upland, the only significant settlement in Pennsylvania. Legend says that coming ashore, Penn asked a companion to rename the settlement, who responded with "Chester." This site is credited with being the first place Penn stepped onto his land grant of Pennsylvania.

Then, the entourage proceeded up the river to where Penn planned to build the "greene country town" of Philadelphia. The *Welcome* anchored near the current Dock Street. Penn's Landing is now a recreation and entertainment area, one of the city's major attractions.

In stark contrast to the two other sites, which are busy and maintained, the Upland (now Chester) site is forlorn. There is a barren small park and an 1882 bicentennial monument marking Penn's arrival. The monument is a five-foot high, three feet by two feet stone with a marble plaque that is oddly askew on the monument. (Actually, the monument has been relocated from its original site at the mouth of Chester Creek, now the site of a cogeneration electrical plant owned by Scott Paper.

The nearby blighted city of Chester magnifies the forlorn state of historic Penn's Landing. Though there are still surviving industries along the Delaware River in the area Around the Delaware Arc, much has been abandoned or torn down.

The location of the monument is the Southeast corner of 2nd (PA 291) and Penn Streets.

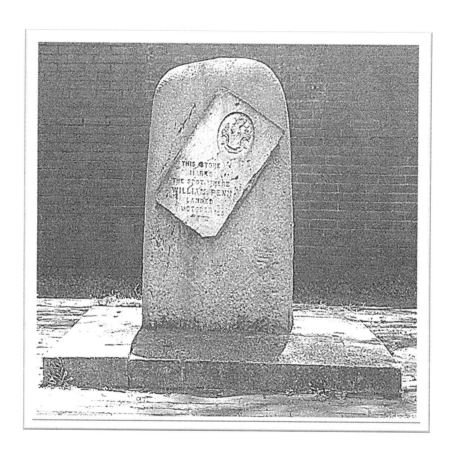

62 - CALEB PUSEY HOUSE

WILLIAM PENN REALIZED THAT FIRST Purchasers who came to his colony would need lumber to build and flour for food, so he engaged his friend Caleb Pusey (1651-1727) to be agent and manager (also 1/32 owner) for Penn's propriety mill to be established along the banks of the Chester Creek at Upland. Pusey travelled with Penn and other Quaker settlers on the *Welcome* in 1682. The makings of Penn's mill were used for the ship's ballast, which Pusey transported overland from Marcus Hook to the fall of Chester Creek. Penn's mill was known as Chester Mills.

Adjacent to the mill site, Penn granted Pusey a hundred acre estate, which Pusey named Langford. On this plantation, Pusey grew food for his family. They spent the first winter in a hastily excavated "pit house." In 1683, he built the first section of the current structure from native stone. The Puseys stayed on the Upland site through 1717, when he and his family moved to East Marlborough Township. (One of his daughter's would become an ancestor to the twentieth century artist, Maxfield Parrish.)

The house and mill had a number of owners through the years, including the Flower family (1792-1845). The Flowers sold the property to the wealthy Chester industrialist, John Price Crozer. (Crozer had a textile mill around the bend of Chester Creek that produced a blue cloth for Union uniforms during the Civil War, to his great profit.) Crozer was a Baptist philanthropist, one of the minor figures in the Layman's Prayer Revival of the mid eighteenth century, but a major benefactor in the Chester area.

Crozer recognized the significance of the Pusey property, where American industry had an early start, if not literally began. He built a wall around the house and gave it over to an African American midwife, whose family lived in it for 60 years. After the Crozer family left Upland, the house once again passed through a succession of families.

In the 1950s, a group of Quaker women initiated a project to restore the house to its original condition. This effort led to the establishment of The Friends of the Caleb Pusey House, which now maintains the house (with Revolutionary War era furniture) and property. The modest grounds have two other buildings: the Crozer Schoolhouse dates from 1849 and the Pennock Log House (c.1765). The log house, built by a Pusey descendent, was removed from Springfield Township and reconstructed on the Chester Creek site.

The property is located at 15 Race Street, Upland, Pennsylvania. New housing on one side and an abandoned industrial area on another, with a couple of residences at the foot of Race Street, an odd setting for such an old and important house. It is the only authenticated house where William Penn visited, not once, but several times.

Though off the usual track for visitors Around the Delaware Arc, the site has much to offer relative to First Purchasers, Pennsylvania's earliest industry, and a late seventeenth century English Vernacular style of architecture.

63 - MARTIN LUTHER KING JR.

MARTIN LUTHER KING JR. (1929-1968) SPENT three formative years (1948 through 1951) at the Crozer Theological Seminary (American Baptist) in Upland, Pennsylvania, an area outside of Chester, Pennsylvania. He graduated from CTS with a Bachelor of Divinity degree.

At the school, he was mentored by a family friend, Rev. J. Pius Barbour of the Calvary Baptist Church (1616 W. 2nd Street Chester). Barbour had particular interest in the small contingent of Crozer's black students, since he was the first African American to graduate from CTS. King was one of 11 black seminarians enrolled at Crozer during those post-war years. He served as student minister at Barbour's church.

King, who at the time was known as Mike, (his birth name was Michael King) graduated first in his class. He was also elected class president.

While at Crozer, he audited classes at the University of Pennsylvania in the philosophy of history, aesthetics, and Immanuel Kant. He studied the Social Gospel movement through the writings of Walter Rauschenbusch, determining that theology could be a basis for human good and progress. But King tempered Rauschenbusch's notion of inevitable progress with Reinhold Niebuhr's more pessimistic view of society. King sided with Niebuhr's contentions that goodness begins with personal transformation through God's grace.

In 1949, King heard a lecture from the executive director of the pacifist organization Fellowship of Reconciliation. King was "deeply moved" but unpersuaded that pacifism was practical. A few months later, King heard a speech on Gandhi at Philadelphia's Fellowship House, a Quaker-rooted inter-faith and inter-racial center in Philadelphia. The speaker was Mordecai Johnson, President of Howard University. King remembered the message as "profound and electrifying," beginning his fascination with Gandhi's non-resistance campaigns.

A Martin Luther King Jr. Commemorative Mural (2009) is painted on the side of the Calvary Baptist Church at 1616 West 2nd Street, in Chester. Additionally, a nearby park at West 6th and Engle Streets is dedicated to Dr. King. The park includes a five-foot high and 685-pound bust of the great civil rights leader. The building of the former Crozer Theological Seminary is located at 21st Street and Upland Avenue, Upland, Pennsylvania.

WEST CHESTER

64 - DOWER HOUSE

IN 1681, A YEAR BEFORE WILLIAM Penn arrived in America, a group of Quakers from northern Wales bought a 40,000 acre tract of land for ten cents an acre. West Chester became the Welsh Tract's shire town. Following the Revolutionary War (1786), the town of West Chester, in the old Welsh Tract at the heart of the region, replaced Chester on the Delaware River as the seat of Chester County.

In 1710 a road was cut, connecting West Chester with Philadelphia. In 1712, on Goshen Road, John and Mary Wall built a two room stone house. After several additions by successive owners, through three centuries, the house has the distinction of being the longest continuously occupied house in West Chester, now a city of some 18,000 residents.

Known as the Dower House, this structure, clad in the region Around the Delaware Arc's characteristic fieldstone, is a good example of the region's "add-on" structures that modified modest-sized colonial homes into larger dwellings suitable for later sensibilities.

In the 1920s and early 1930s, the Dower House was thoroughly renovated in the Colonial Revival style by a prominent architect R. Brognard Okie. Okie was known for his meticulous preservation work. At the time, the house was owned by Joseph and Dorothy Hergesheimer. Hergesheimer (1880-1954) was a prominent writer of the early twentieth century and a bon-vivant, who with his diminutive, gentian-eyed wife, were famous for their parties.

Born in Philadelphia to a middle class family, Hergesheimer wrote novels about the manners of the upper class. His best-known work was *Three Black Pennys* (1917), which chronicled three fictional generations of Pennsylvania ironmasters. From 1914 through 1934, Hergesheimer wrote twenty novels.

With scant plot but strong characterization, written in what he called an "aesthetic" style but which critics labeled as "florid," his books were popular and a few became movies. (Lillian Gish starred in the film version of *Three Black Pennies*.) He became wealthy, buying the eight room Dower House, renovating it in the popular Colonial Revival style, filling it with a collection of art, including period glass, and maintaining a staff to manage the house's affairs.

At the Dower House, the Hergesheimers entertained literary luminaries of the era, including H.L. Mencken and Sinclair Lewis. Hergesheimer invited Lewis to live in West Chester, while he was working on the manuscript of *Main Street* (1920). After a few weeks, Lewis left, protesting West Chester was too active.

In a 1925 tongue-in-cheek letter, D.H. Lawrence mentioned the Hergesheimers and their forthcoming book about the house's history and restoration. Lawrence declared that

he was glad he did not have to write about the New Mexican cabin he was living in; it would only amount to four pages.

Carl Van Vechten, a frequent visitor to the Dower House in the 1920s, remembered the "drunken twenties" and credited Hergesheimer with almost singlehandedly inventing the Daiquiri cocktail, at least introducing the Cuban drink to his literati friends and the bars he frequented.

More so than most houses of the region Around the Delaware Arc, the Dower House (100 Goshen Road) has a public personality. It also has its own "autobiography."

Hergesheimer fell out of popular literary favor and into obscurity in the early 1930s. Unable to afford the life to which he had become accustomed, he became more abrasive and publicly dour.

He sold Dower House and most of its contents in 1945 and moved to New Jersey. Yet his affection for West Chester endured. His body is buried in a local cemetery.

The Dower House is located at 100 East Goshen Road, West Chester.

65 - HORACE PIPPIN

THE ARTIST HORACE PIPPIN STANDS out among the celebrated painters of the region Around the Delaware Arc.

Pippin was born in 1888, in West Chester, Chester County, Pennsylvania. He spent much of his youth in Goshen, New York. Before enlisting in the Army in 1917, he worked at various odd jobs. He fought in France, a member of the celebrated all-black 369th Infantry Regiment. Less than a month before the Armistice, a sniper severely wounded him in the right shoulder. With a disability pension, he returned to West Chester with wife and son, where he spent the remainder of his years.

In his early years, Pippin had enjoyed drawing. As a boy, he won a box of crayons in a drawing contest. He drew scenes of horse racing in Goshen during his youth and sketched during his Army service. Post-war, he began to paint, in part to rehabilitate his dominant right arm that had been wounded in the war. He first used the technique of burning images into a wood panel and filling in the outline. By the mid-1920s, he had begun to use oils.

His relatively small paintings, thick with paint, attracted attention beyond West Chester, including the famous Philadelphia collector Albert F. Barnes. (Barnes included Pippin alongside the great French Impressionist artists in his celebrated personal collection.) Pippin was mostly self-taught, though in the 1940s he took a few courses at The Barnes.

He painted what he had experienced during the War, the domestic life of African Americans with which Pippin was familiar, history related to the African American experience, Christian religious themes, and Chester County vignettes. Pippin occasionally referenced earlier area artists including Edward Hick's "Peaceable Kingdom" variations and Benjamin West's "Penn's Treaty with the Indians."

He once told a friend, "[Y]ou know why I am great?…Because I paint things exactly the way they are….I don't do what these white guys do. I don't go around here making up a whole lot of stuff. I paint it exactly the way it is and exactly the way I see it."

Pippin was not particularly political, yet by subject and execution his work unmistakably spoke of the African American experience of the first half of the twentieth century. His domestic scenes project a dignified domesticity. His historical scenes, of Abraham Lincoln and John Brown, remember the struggle against slavery. His two portraits of Marian Anderson speak to contemporary struggles for egalitarianism. His religious works evoke the universal theme of suffering. These transcendent themes and their honest portrayal elevate Pippin among artists who practiced Around the Delaware Arc.

Horace Pippin died in 1946.

66 - LAFAYETTE'S TRIUMPHANT VISIT TO WEST CHESTER

ONE OF THE GRANDEST EVENTS of Chester County, Pennsylvania history occurred during the triumphant, commemorative 1824-1825 grand tour of the Marquis de Lafayette. The United States Congress, via President Monroe, had invited Lafayette to visit all the twenty-four states. The Brandywine Battlefield sites had particular meaning for Lafayette. Not only was it his first battle, he sustained a leg wound, in the vicinity of Birmingham Meeting House.

With his son George Washington Lafayette, the Marquis entered Chester County in July 1825. His party first visited Chadds Ford and then proceeded to the Gilpin House a mile further north. Lafayette greeted the aged and ill Gideon Gilpin, whose home he had made his pre-battle headquarters.

Via Painter's Crossroad, Lafayette and his entourage went to Dilworthtown, where a large group of celebrants greeted him. Turning toward the main battlefield, as they approached the Birmingham Meeting House, Lafayette stopped the carriage and in French, described to his son how the battle had moved across the landscape, including a nearby spot where he had been wounded. Another contingent met them at the Birmingham Meeting House. Along the way they stopped for lunch at Samuel Jones's mansion beyond the Meetinghouse. They passed through Strode's Mill and Darlington Woods, nearing West Chester.

When the contingent reached West Chester, a 13-gun salute was fired and local volunteer troops joined Lafayette's group, making an impressive entourage. The procession entered West Chester at High Street where an enormous crowd waited. Contemporaries estimated 10,000 citizens standing and cheering along the route. The parade snaked through West Chester streets: High to Market to Walnut to Gay to High to Market to Church to Gay to High. At High Street, the troops assembled in a large field and received Lafayette's favorable review. A reception and dinner for forty followed in the Court House with many toasts, much music, and a couple of short speeches.

The evening ended with a song sung to the familiar tune "Auld Lang Syne," beginning:

Should days of trial be forgot,
Although those days have fled?
Can we neglect the sacred spot
Where patriot heroes blood shed?

Ah, no! those days of auld lang syne
We can never forget.
When with our sires to Brandywine
Came gallant Lafayette.

Taylor's monument to the memory of Lafayette

67 - SERPENTINE BUILDINGS

SERPENTINE, A LIGHT-OLIVE GREEN colored rock, appears in several areas of Chester County, Pennsylvania. When near the surface, the toxic minerals of the rock create unique ecosystems known as serpentine barrens. Additionally, veins of serpentine have been quarried, particularly in the eighteenth and nineteenth centuries, when this soft stone was sawn into rectangular blocks. One of the most productive of Southeastern Pennsylvania serpentine quarries was known as Brinton's Quarries, some three miles south of West Chester on Birmingham Road, southeast of its intersection with Street Road.

The distinctive green rock was first quarried in the 1730s. Many buildings that survive in the area surrounding Brandywine Battlefield are constructed of blocks of serpentine. (The largest block taken from a Brinton quarry was 16 feet by three feet square.) Additionally, the area has several serpentine Victorian buildings, including Edgewood on Birmingham Road south of Birmingham Meeting House.

Also known as the Sharpless House for its first owner Charles Sharpless, Edgewood sits atop Birmingham Hill, a 1777 battle site between British and American troops. The original house (1845) combined Gothic Revival architecture with local Quaker influences. The house passed through several families, including the wealthy Biddles of Philadelphia. In 1889, the Biddles added a large tower to provide their servants back stairs to the family floors. Biddle women kept their jewels in a basement "safe room." The locals referred to the structure with its new tower as Biddles' Castle.

Legend holds that a secret basement room harbored fugitive slaves, a plausible story because the Sharpless family was Quaker.

Birmingham Road, Brinton Bridge Road, Meetinghouse Road, and Wylie Road all have Pennsylvania Scenic By-Way status. Among the sights to behold on these roads around Brandywine Battlefield are distinctive serpentine buildings made of locally quarried stone.

68 - GREAT MINQUA PATH

THE LENNI LENAPE, THE NATIVE Americans of the Brandywine Valley, called the Native Americans to the immediate west by a name (Minqua) that meant "treacherous." Seventeenth century Europeans knew the Minqua as the Susquehannock for their homeland along the Susquehanna River and also as Conestoga, for the location of one of their important villages (and last village) in the early eighteenth century.

The Minqua, an Iroquois people, controlled lands rich in beaver along the lower Susquehanna Valley. Via an 80-mile long path, they established a fur trade with a succession of European interests that contended to control the lands along the Delaware River: the Swedes, the Dutch, and finally the English. During the era of Swedish and Dutch control of the Delaware River region, the Minqua followed Beaversrede (Beaver Road) to Fort Beaversrede (current Philadelphia) along the lower Schuylkill River.

During the first half of the seventeenth century, the Minqua conquered the Lenni Lenape who lived along this route, making them subservient to Minqua rule. When the Minqua were conquered by the Iroquois (1662) the Lenni Lenape became subservient to the Iroquois.

The Minqua Path is remembered by two adjacent historical markers in West Chester (Wilmington Pike or Route 202 and Church Avenue) and by a handsome monument with a life-size beaver sculpture at Rose Valley (Rose Valley Road a half mile south of Moylan).

U.S. Route 30, the famous Lincoln Highway, roughly follows the Great Minqua Path. More specifically, PA Route 162, the Strasburg Road, follows the path through Chester County.

DELAWARE COUNTY

69 - CHEYNEY UNIVERSITY

ALONG THE CHESTER COUNTY AND Delaware County border, north of Route 1, is Cheyney University, the oldest of the historically American black colleges. It owes its origin, as do many of the institutions of the region Around the Delaware Arc, to a Quaker sensibility for social justice and philanthropy.

In Philadelphia, the decade of the 1820s brought increasing conflict between immigrants (particularly the Irish, but Germans, too) and free African Americans along with their antislavery allies. The tensions broke out in riots.

Increasing industrialization, diminishing the need for artisans and journeymen, resulted in competition for unskilled factory jobs, aggravating economic tensions that already existed among ethnicities. African Americans sunk to the bottom of the labor pool.

Richard Humphreys (1750–1832), a Philadelphia Quaker, witnessed the racial strife and economic plight of African American laborers. In his will (dictated in 1829, the year of a significant riot), he bequeathed a tenth of his estate, 10,000 dollars, to establish a school to train blacks: an institution: "...to instruct the descendants of the African Race in school learning, in the various branches of the mechanic Arts, trades and Agriculture, in order to prepare and fit and qualify them to act as teachers…." He charged 13 fellow Quakers to design and establish this pioneering school.

The school began (1837) in Philadelphia as the African Institute, but soon changed its name to Institute for Colored Youth. In 1902, the

Institute moved to its current location, when it bought Quaker George Cheyney's farm. In 1913, the college adopted the State's "teacher college" curricula, changing its name to Cheyney State Teachers College. In 1959, it became Cheyney State College and in 1983, Cheyney University of Pennsylvania.

Today, this liberal arts college has 1,700 students. Through its years, it has graduated some 10,000 students, mostly African Americans, though today it attracts a racial and ethnic diversity.

Its 275-acre campus features an historic quadrangle with structures dating to its first decade, including a recently refurbished, fieldstone Humphrey's Hall.

The campus is located off Cheyney Road: 1837 University Circle, West Chester.

70 - NEWLIN GRIST MILL

THROUGH THE MIDDLE OF THE nineteenth century, industry Around the Delaware Arc was largely powered by water. Throughout Chester and Delaware Counties, Pennsylvania and New Castle County, Delaware creeks tumbled from the descending Piedmont toward the Delaware River.

A handful of mill buildings have survived, most converted for contemporary use, such as the Hedgerow Theater (gristmill and bobbin factory, Rose Valley) and the Brandywine Museum (gristmill).

A Delaware County working gristmill, Newlin Grist Mill, has been meticulously restored. It sits in the midst of 150 acres along the West Branch of the Chester Creek (south of Route 1). The first mill on the site dates from 1704. The Newlin family replaced the first building with two other mills during their 113 years of ownership. With subsequent changes of ownership, the third mill operated through 1941. During its active operation, the mill ground wheat, corn, oats, buckwheat, and rye.

A ninth generation descendent of the original Newlins bought the property in 1957 and established a foundation to restore and maintain the mill as a museum. Today, several other buildings complete the historic tableau of a representative mill site.

Despite its proximity to busy Route 1 (Baltimore Pike), with development along Cheyney Road to the south, the setting is tranquil and evocative of the nineteenth century, particularly the mill machinery. A waterwheel turns water rushing over its top from a millrace. An impressive group of gears harness the power of a single turning axle at the hub of the waterwheel.

The Newlin Grist Mill is a welcoming place and friendly to visitors. Tables invite picnicking, benches are arranged to appreciate the landscape, and trout fishing (for a fee) is child friendly.

It is located two miles east of Routes 1 and 202, at 219 South Cheyney Road, Glen Mills, Pennsylvania.

71 - JOHN J. TYLER ARBORETUM

THE JOHN J. TYLER ARBORETUM is an extraordinary 650 acre property, situated in Delaware County, Pennsylvania, northwest of Media. This area is remarkably undeveloped thanks to the holdings of the Arboretum and adjacent Ridley Creek State Park.

In 1681, William Penn conveyed the Arboretum property to a fellow English Quaker, Thomas Minshall. The property stayed in a family line (Minshall/Painter/Tyler) through eight generations (1681 through 1944). For much of that time the land was farmed.

In 1825, two bachelor brothers, Minshall (1801) and Jacob Painter (1814), who managed the family farm, began a private arboretum that would grow into a collection of a thousand plants and shrubs. Today, 20 of those original plantings survive and include a few, so-called

state champions. A massive sequoia may be the largest such specimen on the East Coast.

The brothers were mid-nineteenth botanist-scientists. They collected, preserved, and cataloged numerous specimens. In 1863, the brothers built their own fieldstone library to house their books, specimens, and scientific equipment. (In season, guided tours are conducted of the library.)

In 1914, John J. Tyler inherited the family property. Upon his death in 1930, his wife Laura Hoopes Tyler left the estate in trust as the John J. Tyler Arboretum. Upon her death in 1944, eight generations of family residency on the property ended.

In 1946, a respected horticulturalist, John C. Wister (1887-1982), became the Arboretum's first director. Wister served as director of both the arboretum and bird sanctuary through 1968. Wister had previously landscaped more than forty acres of Swarthmore College's arboretum-like campus. With his wife Gertrude Smith, they added collections and began the maintenance of the wooded area surrounding the buildings and gardens. (Wister was 73 when he married Gertrude, who was also a horticulturalist.) The "Wister Collection" of flowering plants and shrubs is an explosion of colorful blooms in spring.

The Arboretum has a Pinetum, a collection of conifer trees, a Native Woodlawn walk featuring trees common to the Northeast, a Fragrant Garden of plants and herbs once visited by Helen Keller, and an educational Meadow Maze. There are a few original buildings in addition to the Painter Library: a restored and repurposed fieldstone bank barn;

Lachford Hall, adapted by successive generations into a Victorian summer home, where the family lived from 1738 through 1937; and a Painter brothers' greenhouse that looks strikingly contemporary. Seven trails, totaling 20 miles, meander through the surrounding woods. The grounds even include a small rare serpentine barrens parcel.

There are many child-friendly features incorporated into the landscape. The three bears' chairs are especially enchanting.

Each year, the staff organizes more than a hundred programs for adults and children.

The entrance to the Arboretum is located at 515 Painter Road, Media.

72 - BOOTHS CORNER FARMER'S MARKET

ONE OF THE HOME GROWN places Around the Delaware Arc, redolent with the aromas and tastes of the region, is Booths Corner Farmers Market, a weekend institution since 1932.

George Phillips, a farmer who owned 13 acres on Naamans Creek Road near the Foulk Road intersection, operated a roadside stand to sell vegetables, fruit, and other foodstuffs. He partnered with Amish farmers from Lancaster and Chester Counties, setting up his large barn as a weekend and seasonal market.

The locals called Phillips's place "The Sale," a rabbit warren of shed-like buildings added to through the years. Aspiring entrepreneurs rented canvas shrouded stalls and sold a hodgepodge of merchandise, such as remaindered paperback books with their covers torn off, 45-rpm records that had gone out of vogue or never had been in vogue, and military surplus. At an intersection of two sections a gnarly little man selling condoms set up a card table upon which sat a worn Kraft paper bag, its top edge turned down in a cuff. He repeated the refrain: "How many, how many, how many...." Another gnarly little man sold bushels of potatoes, tomatoes, peppers, cucumbers and such at the main entrance, pouring the product from basket into a paper bag. He became what is now known as the *avatar* of The Sale. He gladly "plugged" a watermelon to offer a taste of it to a customer who was considering it. The Amish presence grew stronger.

By the post-war period, in good weather, beneath strings of naked light bulbs at the main entrance, barkers hawked their varied products from the back of carnival trailers, entertainers entertained (including a young Bill Haley), and an "auction" sold merchandise from the back of a flatbed trailer. (The "auction" anticipated the contemporary QVC channel in nearby West Chester.)

The Sale burned to the ground in 1973. It was rebuilt in a much more organized and expanded form. It seems more sanitary, less gritty, too. There is no longer a weekend mini-carnival in the parking lot—no snake oil barkers, no candy apples or popcorn, no snow cones stands

Yet, if you want a visceral experience of the region Around the Delaware Arc, including a glimpse of "real" people, Booths Corners Farmers Market is the place to visit on Friday or Saturday, any weekend throughout the year.

The Market's location is 1362 Naamans Creek Road, Garnet Valley.

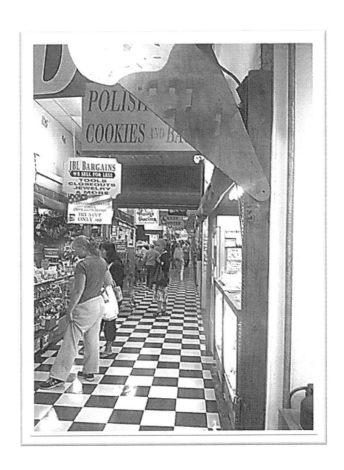

73 - BILL HALEY

ONE OF THE EARLY FIGURES in Rock 'n Roll was Bill Haley (1925-1981), who with the group Bill Haley and His Comets sang "Crazy, Man, Crazy" (1952), the first song of a new genre to hit the popular music charts. "Rock Around the Clock" (1956) became his signature song, the anthem of a new musical era. Other hits followed, including "See You Later, Alligator" and "Shake, Rattle and Roll."

From the age of seven, Haley lived in Boothwyn on Meetinghouse Road in Delaware County, Pennsylvania. He attended the nearby Chelsea School, dropping out of after eighth grade, at the age of 15 (1940).

According to a boyhood acquaintance, Haley had a bad eye, carried around a guitar slung over his shoulder, and had the reputation of being a hillbilly. Perhaps the distinctive curl reaching down his forehead was an attempt to disguise his bad eye. An early, if not first, performance took place at the then very gritty Booths Corner Farmers Market at Foulk and Naamans Creek Roads.

When he was starting out as a country western singer, he and his band (Bill Haley's Saddlemen) played as many local bars and other venues as possible, supplementing Haley's paltry salary from a Chester radio station, where he deejayed and was program manager. His band's music evolved from western swing to rock 'n roll, changing their name to the Comets, a play on the once a century Halley's Comet.

When Bill Haley and His Comets made it big, Haley purchased a house on Foulk Road north of Booths Corner, a low ranch set back from the highway. He parked his pink Cadillac kin the driveway, often his bandmates' Cadillacs in a variety of colors were parked there too. On clement days, the Comets might be seen practicing in the front yard of the house Haley called Melody Manor, six Cadillacs in six colors lining the long driveway.

He lost the home in 1960, the victim of an unscrupulous business manager. The ranch home looks much as it did a half century ago, just north of Bethel Road on Foulk Road. The current owners have erected an ersatz street sign: "Melody Lane."

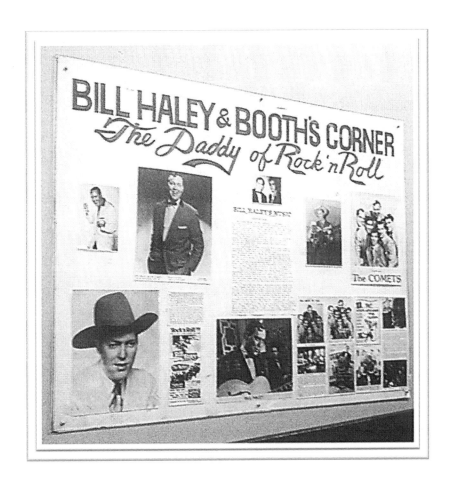

74 - A TALE OF TWO CHURCHES

THERE ARE TWO METHODIST CHURCHES on Foulk Road (Route 261) on either side of the Delaware Arc, within a mile of each other.

The Delaware Church is now known as Chester Bethel, the oldest Methodist congregation continuously gathered in Delaware, its origins preceding the Revolutionary War. It first met in a number of local houses, including Robert Cloud's house. In 1789, a log structure, Cloud's Chapel, was erected. In 1799, a stone church named Bethel Chapel replaced the log chapel. In 1809 and 1810, the famous circuit rider Francis Asbury visited the congregation, calling their building a "beautiful new house." A much grander two-story brick structure with a serpentine front replaced the smaller building in 1873. The congregation adopted the name Chester Bethel.

One hundred years later, on a nearby plot, the congregation built a modern 1972 structure, leaving the 1873 edifice standing. (It now houses a large thrift store and is known as the "Old Serpentine Church.")

In the mid-nineteenth century, a controversy caused a schism of membership. Ostensibly, it involved singing. The split followed the line between older and younger members. The younger faction introduced a new hymnal, an 1849 edition of "The Lute of Zion." The minister and the older contingent opposed what they considered "sacrilegious innovation." One older member declared, "Anybody with common sense ought to know that it will not help the voice to look when you sing upon those things you call keys and bars, with black and white tadpoles, some with their tails up, some with their tails down, decorated with flags and trying to crawl through the fence. It's all the work of the Devil."

The church temporarily closed. New trustees won election. The congregation split. The older members eventually built their own church less than a mile away in Pennsylvania, naming it Siloam. They completed their new building in 1853.

In 1867, the Siloam congregation played a significant role in founding The Brandywine Summit Camp Meeting in nearby Concord Township on a site known as Johnson's Woods.

The camp continues to represent the post-Civil War Methodist Camp Movement. Brandywine Summit Camp remains a summer place of architecturally significant, nineteenth century cottages. Worship and lectures take place in an open-side, covered amphitheater in season.

Today, the two congregations on Foulk Road, within a mile of one another, hold occasional joint services.

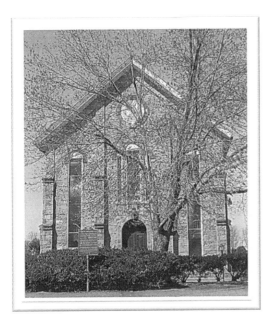

75 - BRANDYWINE SUMMIT CAMP MEETING

THE SECOND GREAT AWAKENING TOOK place from the 1790s through the 1840s. The Methodists and Baptists, and also the Presbyterians emphasized an enthusiastic style of worship. On the frontier, folks traveled miles to gather in great camp gatherings and listen to itinerant preachers sermonize throughout several days that might stretch into a week and longer. The camp meetings were often little carnivals, too. Drinking, dancing, lively music, and licentious behavior often erupted at these temporary meeting grounds. These three denominations, in their various expressions, experienced considerable growth.

Following the ecclesiastical tribulations of the Civil War that had split denominations along Union and Confederate lines, several denominations strove to heal and renew themselves and society. Among the Methodists,

one strategy was called the American Methodist Camp Meeting Movement. Among its objectives was the renewal of the family, as well as the renewal of the soul. For Methodists, the target audience was a rising middle-class, possibly displaced from rural roots, who wanted relatively economical summer escapes from hot, dirty, and unwholesome city life—at the same time stirring memories of old time religion and rural life of the beginning of the century.

What Presbyterians had initiated in the post-Civil War camp meeting movement, peppery Methodist preachers turned into their own beloved summer gatherings. Rather than tents, when the meetings institutionalized, small cottages sprouted up.

Around the Delaware Arc, one such place is the Brandywine Summit Camp Meeting. In 1865, a preacher from the Siloam Church near Booths Corners held a summer prayer meeting in Johnson's Wood. The William Johnson farmhouse still stands on the Wilmington Pike (Route 202) and Beaver Valley Road. The following year, seven other Wilmington churches joined the Siloam congregation.

Imagine the romantic, though primitive, setting: a knocked together pulpit and mourners' bench, illuminated pots of pitch and resin placed on mounds of earth, and over it all a great piece of canvas for shelter.

Brandywine Summit has held a summer camp meeting every year since 1865, incorporating as an Association in 1884. Charter rules prohibited the cutting of trees, hence, today, a few houses have accommodated growing trees and tall trees shelter the cottages and tabernacle.

Today, nearly 70 simple, mostly one-story cottages survive, many with front porches where campers meet and greet one another. An open sided tabernacle (dating from 1884) remains the center of the community, and the camp's avenues spoke out from this center. The avenues carry the names of founding churches: Siloam, Elam, Lebanon, Summit, Union, Brandywine, Asbury, Scott, and St. Paul's.

The Association has beloved community-creating traditions, including an end of season "Walk Around," when after a concluding concert, the campers promenade along the avenues, singing hymns.

Brandywine Summit Camp Meeting perches on the edge of Chateau Country, providing a contrast of lifestyles and intentions to country manors and their landed estates.

The Camp's entrance is west of Route 202 (Wilmington Pike) at 119 Beaver Valley Rd, Chadds Ford.

REGIONALISMS

76 – PIEDMONT

THE LANDSCAPE OF THE REGION Around the Delaware Arc is perched at the edge of the Piedmont. *Piedmont*, from the French, means *foothills*.

This Piedmont is part of the great chain of the ancient Appalachian Mountains. A few miles south of the Delaware Arc, the Piedmont dips below the Coastal Plain. The Coastal Plain is a flat and short approach to the Delaware River.

The course that follows the Piedmont meeting the Coastal Plain is known as the *fall line*. West of Wilmington the Kirkwood Highway, (Route 2) generally follows the Fall Line.

The major streams Around the Delaware Arc, Chester Creek, White Clay Creek, Red Clay Creek, and especially Brandywine Creek have falling waters, important in the Colonial and Early Republic eras for the water power that drove hundreds of mills of various sorts: snuff, paper, grains, textiles, lumber, and black powder begin the list. The many creeks provided ample water for heavy forests and fruitful agriculture.

For more than 235 million years, after the expansion of Appalachian system ended, the Piedmont has been eroding. This long epoch of erosion sculpted the graceful contours of the landscape Around the Delaware Arc. The surface rocks are weathered and in various stages of decomposition. Erosion and sedimentation deposited the fertile soils. As the upper layers wore away, buried strata of rock rose toward the surface

The time-shaped landscape Around the Delaware Arc has recognized aesthetic appeal.

It evokes memories of an agricultural heritage from the late seventeenth, throughout the eighteenth, and into the early nineteenth century. It also evokes industries powered by water and the relatively simple technologies of mills. And it evokes a truly ancient geology from half a billion years ago plus a relentless evolution.

The aesthetic of the Piedmont region Around the Delaware Arc is complex phenomenon, a continuing saga that began 500 million years ago and continues.

77 - BLUE ROCK

BENEATH WILMINGTON AND CLIMBING INTO the Piedmont is a famous rock, a kind of granite known generically as *Wilmington blue rock* or Brandywine *blue granite* and more formally as *Wilmington blue gneiss*. Granite is a *gneiss*, a metaphoric rock composed of four primary minerals: quartz, feldspar, pyroxene, and magnetite. Some specimens of the granite also sometime contain orthopyrxene and/or garnet.

The granite had its origins 570 million years ago at the root of a massive volcano. Geological forces (seaward volcanos crashing into a continental land mass) thrust the original minerals 7 to 13 miles deep below the adjacent continent. Tremendous pressures and heat over millions of years metamorphosed those original materials. When uplifted and cooled during later cataclysmic mountain building (orogeny) of

what became the Appalachian Range, the recrystallized rock we know had formed. The Appalachian Range stabilized 250 million years ago. Since then, erosion has removed 7 to 13 miles of surface to the level of the granite, which also rebounded as the upward weight was removed.

From south of Rockland to Wilmington's Market Street Bridge, the Brandywine Creek has cut a gorge, a winding four mile stretch, with a fall of some one-hundred twenty feet. Natural, weathered granite walls define the gorge. The course of the Creek is studded with granite boulders

Falling water, in the seventeenth through the nineteenth centuries powered some 150 mills, along the Brandywine, including the famous du Pont powder mills, whose buildings were constructed from Wilmington blue granite, a handy, durable, and attractive building material.

When first quarried or a boulder is split, the granite it is often a remarkable blue color.

The effects of weather render Brandywine blue granite a dark gray that often has lighter bands undulating through it from gray to white. The bands trace its ancient metamorphosis.

78 - RUBBLE STONE CONSTRUCTION

IN CHESTER COUNTY, PENNSYLVANIA THE eighteenth century buildings—whether Penn Plan Houses or Pennsylvania Bay Barns—often were built of fieldstone, masoned together in a motley pattern of irregular weathered rocks, usually of several hues of reddish brown. The coloration of the ancient metamorphoric fieldstone rocks was a result of iron content. Less frequently, these old buildings were constructed from shades of gray granite.

The term "rubble stone construction" describes such organic buildings (in the sense they come from and seem part of the landscape), literally clad in surface and stream rocks easily accessed or at hand from field-clearing. These rocks may have been shaped a little to fit together with adjacent rocks. Rubble walls are called uncoursed. (Coursed walls have been quarried and blocked.)

Later artists and architects of the region used rubble construction as grounding for their newer forms. Artist Wharton Esherick (1887-1970) began his career in Will Price's Rose Valley. (He served as set designer for the Hedgerow Theater.) He established his own home and studio in Malvern, now open to the public.

Wharton is considered by many scholars to be the major transitional figure from the American Craftsman movement of the turn of the century and the mid-century Studio Furniture Movement. The buildings on his property are fine examples of traditional Chester and Delaware Counties' rubble construction adapted to contemporary artistic sensibilities.

79 – SERPENTINE

ONE OF THE DISTINCTIVE FEATURES Around the Delaware Arc is stone—the solid granite along the Brandywine Creek as the waters approach Wilmington, the multihued fieldstone houses and barns from the eighteenth century, the orderly blue-hued walls flowing over the hills of Chateau Country, and now and again, a serpentine faced structure, dating to the eighteenth and early nineteenth century. These green structures stand out because of their unusual color.

Serpentine is an olive green in color and may have a scaly appearance, hence its name meaning "snakelike." It is a soft sedimentary stone often compared to limestone. Its softness and ease of cutting made it popular for local buildings, yet the same features render it vulnerable to weathering and the acidic air of industrialization.

Serpentine resulted from elements and minerals deposited in an ancient ocean, the activities of volcanoes, and tectonic forces that separated continents, burying, heating, and thrusting strata over hundreds of million years.

In Chester County, Pennsylvania, deposits of serpentine are lifted to a few feet below ground. A toxic mix of metals (including nickel, chromium, and especially magnesium) and a surface that quickly heats to the sun result in a unique environment, micro ecosystems that early residents contrasted to the otherwise fertile landscape. They named these parched patches "barrens."

Northwest of the Arc are surviving serpentine barrens, the largest along the East coast. For example near Nottingham, Pennsylvania, the Nottingham Barrens (open to the public) offer 630 acres of an accessible miniature ecosystem with rare plants and animals. There are serpentine barrens at the ChesLens Preserve along the West Branch of the Brandywine Creek. And the Tyler Arboretum has Delaware County's only serpentine barrens. Three, long abandoned serpentine quarries are located on Brinton Road, a few miles south of West Chester.

80 - LENNI LENAPE

WHEN EUROPEANS ARRIVED IN THE seventeenth century, the Lenni Lenape inhabited the region Around the Delaware Arc. This Algonquin speaking group of Native Americans extended from contemporary New York State to where the Delaware River met the Atlantic Ocean. There were three Lenni Lenape subgroups, including the Unami, (People down the River). The Unami's homeland included what is now Southeastern Pennsylvania and Northern Delaware. They referred to this homeland as *Lenapehoking* (Land of the Lenape).

The Lenni Lenape called themselves *men of men*, often translated as *original people*. Among other indigenous groups of Algonquin people, they were considered to be a grandfather tribe which afforded them particular respect. They were known for their diplomacy in the settling of disputes. The early Europeans found them to be remarkably hospitable.

The Lenni Lenape lived in groups upward of a few hundred persons. They hunted and fished, of course; but they also cultivated crops: corn, squash, beans, sweet potatoes, and tobacco. They moved from camp to camp throughout the year depending on the growing season.

It is estimated that the three groupings of the Lenni Lenape totaled 20,000 at the beginning of the seventeenth century. The Swedes and Finns arrived in 1638, initiating European contact with the Lenni Lenape and beginning a remarkably quick decline of these indigenous people. Much of the decline involved devastations of European diseases.

Another factor in the decline of the Lenni Lenape involved the Susquehannock (Minqua) who established an 80-mile trail from the Chesapeake region to the Schuylkill River to trade furs with the Europeans. Minqua, whom the Lenni Lenape called "treacherous," were Iroquois speaking. From 1630 through 1635, the Minqua warred with the Lenni Lenape and subdued them. When the Iroquois subsequently defeated the Minqua, the Lenni Lenape fell under Iroquois control.

By William Penn's 1683 arrival, the Lenni Lenape had been reduced to perhaps 4,000. Penn was scrupulous regarding the sale of Native American occupied lands. He sought to establish treaties for the conveyance of land, the first a mythic "Great Treaty," in 1682 at the village of Shackamaxon near Philadelphia. This event was immortalized by a Benjamin West 1771 painting and a number of mid-nineteenth portrayals by Edward Hicks.

Penn's scrupulous dealings with the Lenni Lenape, after his 1718 death, did not continue among his heirs. By the 1740's, the Lenni Lenape were prohibited from planting corn; and their claim to a promised reservation along the West Branch of the Brandywine was not honored.

Remnant groups migrated west to Ohio and north to New York and Quebec. A Lenni Lenape woman born in 1730, Hannah Freeman, also known as Indian Hannah, upon her death in 1803, was considered the last Lenni Lenape in the region Around the Delaware Arc.

While a number of places bear names that harken back to original Algonquin names, the Quakers named their Meeting House by names that were not "heathen" in origin, thereby further diminishing the original Lenni Lenape presence.

81 - INDIAN HANNAH

INDIAN HANNAH, WHO DIED IN the Chester County Poorhouse in 1802, is considered to be the last Lenni Lenape to live in Chester County, Pennsylvania. The narrative of her life is a significant piece of the mythos of the region Around the Delaware Arc, conveying a romanticized version of the relationship of Europeans with the Native Americans

By the year of her birth, 1730 or 1731, the Lenni Lenape had been dramatically reduced in numbers by tribal wars and European-introduced disease. Many had migrated to what would become New York and Ohio and also to Canada.

Born in Kennett, Chester County, Pennsylvania on the William Webb Place, her extended family included her mother and father, two younger siblings, a grandmother, and two aunts. In the spring, her mother and family took the family to Newlin, some ten miles distant, to grow corn. When the Lenni Lenape were banned from growing corn in Chester County, her father and two of his sons went to Shamokin (some 100 miles distant). The women of the family stayed behind (indicating a matrilineal society). The women established another cabin near Centerville in New Castle County, Delaware. For a few years, they moved back and forth between Kennett and Centerville. Following a notorious massacre of twenty Susquehannock in 1763 (near Lancaster) by the Paxton Boys, Indian Hannah with grandmother Indian Jane and mother Indian Sarah spent seven years with fellow Lenni Lenapes in New Jersey. The women returned to Chester County, their homeland; in this fashion, by their presence, these women reclaimed land along the Brandywine they believed their native land as well as to be treaty-promised.

When all her close relatives had died, Hannah returned to Kennett, which served as a base for her own peripatetic (perhaps migratory) ways that increased as she aged. She worked as a seamstress, wove baskets, bound brooms, and gathered medicinal herbs. She sold these products on her travels, staying longest where she was most wanted. Her assimilation into European culture had caused her to declare that she had "almost forgot to talk Indian." She further mused that she no longer liked "their [Indians'] manner of living so well as the white peoples."

In her later years, she was a familiar sight to many, riding or walking beside her horse, accompanied by two dogs, Elmun and Putome, which she commanded by the word, "Cotch-a-mingo," and by her pigs. She grew more eccentric as she aged, becoming childish, meddlesome, and troublesome. Several caring friends managed to have her admitted to a new Chester County Poorhouse in Embreeville (ironically, she may have been the first resident, 1801) She died in 1802.

A memorial marker for Indian Hannah is located on Route 162 about 100 yards north of Corcoran's Bridge at ChesLen Preserve. Another memorial for Indian Hannah, signifying her birth site, is attached to a boulder on Route 52 a tenth of a mile north of Route 1.

From a contemporary perspective, Indian Hannah kept a tenacious yet fragile hold on tribal land through her peripatetic travels, while also testifying by her presence to treaties made by Penn and his interests—treaties eventually reneged upon.

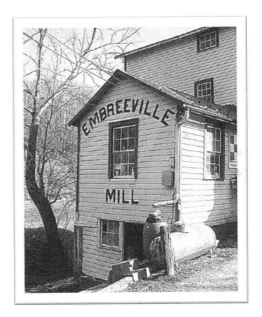

82 - HORSE COUNTRY

NORTH OF KENNETT SQUARE, PENNSYLVANIA, and south of the West Branch of the Brandywine Creek is Chester County's horse country. The name is a nod to the recreation of the wealthy of foxhunting and steeplechase racing (point-to-point). Yes, the hunt continues: packs of carefully bred and trained hounds, leading riders in livery mounted on pedigreed horses, under the authority of a Hunt Master. Point-to-point racing is a relatively common event and has become a public spectacle.

The village of Unionville on Route 82 sits in the center. In all directions, a landscape of deeply sculpted fields rise and fall, the contours subtly accentuated by post and rail fences delineating ownership of hundreds, even thousands of acres—great plots of land that were once (or still are) owned by the wealthy of Wilmington (du Pont) and Philadelphia (Strawbridge). An informal but persuasive culture of horses and open field riding resulted in a preservation ethic embedded in that unique lifestyle.

In the mid-twentieth century, those who loved the hunt began to devise strategies to knit together vast acreage to be able to continue to ride freely and widely in pursuit of the fox. For example, Lammot du Pont did not want his 5,000-acre Buck and Doe Farm to be entangled in taxes, so, in 1943, he sold his farm to Texan Robert Kleberg, who for the next four decades shipped his King Ranch cattle north to fatten before market. Kleberg allowed the hunt to pass through this property, building jumps along the many cattle fences.

When Kleberg's heirs were considering dividing and developing their inheritance, circa 1980, they were convinced by the foxhunting interests to put easements on deeds that restricted future development. This became the pattern for subsequent land sales in this area. New owners, unfamiliar with the ethos of the hunt, also were schooled in the ways of hounds and horses, encouraged to put panels in their fences to allow for passage from field to field.

The landscape remained free from sub-division development, in conjunction with conservation, as well as preservation, interests. The Brandywine Conservancy has led the way, for example, heading efforts to conserve the former King Ranch property as part of the Brandywine Creek Watershed that supplies Wilmington with drinking water. Through conversation easements and a few land gifts, the Brandywine Conservancy has permanently protected some 45,000 acres in the area.

A public parcel of 1,263 aces of this horse country can be accessed at the ChesLen Preserve, a combination of Chester County parkland and a section of what was earlier Buck and Doe Farm and later King Ranch. Two miles of the West Branch of the Brandywine Creek run through the Preserve. It also has serpentine barrens with rare wild plants.

The entrance to the preserve is 1199 Cannery Road, Kennett Square, Pennsylvania.

83 - MUSHROOM FARMS

MUSHROOMS ARE A LATECOMER TO the agriculture Around the Delaware Arc. The industry had its start in Kennett Square, Pennsylvania at the turn of the century. In the mid-1880s, a pair of Quakers from the area imported mushroom spawn from England and experimented in growing mushrooms.

One farmer, William Swayne, already grew carnations for market in elevated beds. He covered the empty space below the carnation beds with burlap. Maintaining the right conditions, the mushrooms thrived. Utilizing proven principles of heat, humidity, and ventilation, Swayne soon erected the first mushroom barn.

With good transportation and nearby markets for the delicate mushroom, the mushroom industry boomed. By 1930, some 500 mushroom houses were growing mushrooms, mostly the popular snowball variety, within ten miles of Kennett Square, growing upwards of 85 percent of the mushrooms consumed in America.

Increasingly the produce was canned and the growers' crops were sent nationwide throughout the entire year. First, imported mushrooms and then a shortage of tin for cans during the Second World War, cut into production. Other areas of the country also began to grow mushrooms, too. Yet Kennett Square continued to account for 60 percent of the nation's mushrooms in the 1970s (perhaps 65 percent today).

The farms are long, low cinderblock buildings traditionally built into a hill. The compost in which the mushrooms are cultivated includes hay, corncobs, chicken manure, and horse manure. (The famed horse country of Chester County is nearby.) In today's mushroom compost, cocoa shells (from Hershey) have been added.

The industry has had certain ethnic distinctions. Many of the early workers were Italian; some would start their own farms. The workers have evolved from local youth both black and white, to Appalachian whites, to African Americans, to Puerto Ricans, and now to Mexicans; the latter represent ninety-eight percent of the current work force.

A famous labor action that began in 1993, "The Kaolin Strike," at the Kennett Square Kaolin Mushroom Farm, helped establish the Mexican laborers' right to unionize and the imperative of the growers to negotiate with the union.

Mushroom farms have consolidated and the smaller growers have gone out of business. (A few Quaker families continue in the industry.) Still the Kennett Square district has sixtysome growers. Production by the remaining farms continues to increase, spurred in part by mushroom types other than the traditional button variety.

Restaurants around the Delaware Arc feature local mushrooms, asserting Kennett Square's reputation as the Mushroom Capital of the World.

Some of the growers offer tours, showing the barns while explaining the art of mushroom cultivation.

84 - PENNSYLVANIA BARN

WILLIAM PENN'S LAND GRANT THAT included Delaware and Chester Counties of Pennsylvania that now border the Delaware Arc, through the mid-nineteenth century, was arguably the most fertile/productive of farm regions in the world. Of course, Quakers established prosperous farms. (A memorable Edward Hicks' painting remembers the lush Quaker farmstead on which he grew up at the turn of the eighteenth into the nineteenth century.)

Penn's remarkable religious tolerance invited industrious German pietist sects to settle in this region. These groups brought their own modest style of German and Swiss barns and replicated them in Pennsylvania.

These European-style early structures evolved into larger and more efficient buildings with distinctive improvements that converged into the *Pennsylvania Barn*. This distinctive style emerged in the late eighteenth century and flourished from the 1820s through 1900. It is easily identified by a few prominent elements.

Such a barn was often built into a hill, its front side or back side beneath ground level, accessing the second floor by an ascending ramp. This is known as *banked*. The front of the Pennsylvania barn has an overhang from the second floor. This seven to eight foot projection is known as a *forebay*. Timber posts or perhaps stone columns support the forebay. It characteristically had a gable roof.

The Pennsylvania Barn evolved for the sake of labor saving efficiency. The second floor had a threshing area, mows along the walls for hay, and a granary often in the overhanging bay. Gravity dropped the hay and grain to the first floor or area under the forebay that accommodated in an orderly fashion, a variety of animals, including cattle, horses, pigs, and sheep.

Delaware and Chester County farms grew oats, corn, and hay to feed the livestock. The primary crop was wheat, which would often make its way to the gristmills along the tumbling waters of the Piedmont's various creeks, including the Brandywine Creek milling district near Wilmington. Brandywine Superfine Flour set a high standard.

The Pennsylvania Barn, because of its banked and fieldstone construction, appears organic to the earth.

Around the Delaware Arc, remaining barns remember the region's agricultural heritage, a convergence of the fertile Piedmont, religious tolerance, an evolving agriculture, and industrious farmers.

85 - SMITH BRIDGE

SMITH BRIDGE ROAD AND RAMSEY Road meet on the east side of the Brandywine at a rare, one-lane, red covered bridge. Bridge 9, popularly known as Smith Bridge, was originally a single span timber covered bridge with stone abutments constructed in 1839.

Vandals burnt it in on the night before Halloween 1962.

The bridge was replaced with a utilitarian structure without sides and a roof. In 2002, the State, with the encouragement of locals (Centerville Civic Association), decided to build a new covered bridge, remembering the 1839 structure, while refurbishing the surviving historic piers and abutments.

The new bridge is made from Bongossi, a rare and expensive African wood that is twice as dense as oak, resistant to fire, decay, and insects.

The 1839 covered bridge was an icon of the Brandywine Valley through 1962. Its twenty-first century replica is equally iconic, possibly the most photographed structure of the region.

86 - CHESTER COUNTY'S QUAKER POET

THOUGH HISTORY IS A CONTINUITY and the region Around the Delaware Arc, from the European perspective, has more than three and a half centuries of evolving habitation, there was a "golden age" from 1790 through 1840, when the fertile Piedmont countryside joined to human industry, made this region the bread-basket of the young Republic. Subsequent sensibilities have long resonated to that era, evoking an emotional response.

For at least 150 years, artists have sought to capture the picturesque aspects of the undulating hills, the pastures and fields, flowing creeks, the fieldstone houses, forebay barns, and the many mills. A recent exhibition at the Brandywine River Museum speculated, "Probably no other place on Earth has been as minutely studied, season after season, as this beautiful stretch of country."

The region has also inspired native writers. Thomas Buchanan Read (1822-1872) and Bayard Taylor (1825-1878) wrote of the lore and landscape around the Brandywine. Arguably, the poet of nineteenth century Chester County, Pennsylvania was John Russell Hayes (1866-1945).

Hayes descended from a long-time Chester County, Pennsylvania Quaker family, who farmed along the Brandywine. Hayes grew up on his parents' Brandywine farm, graduated from Quaker Swarthmore College (1888), and married (1892) a Swarthmore classmate from Wilmington. He graduated from the Law school of the University of Pennsylvania, but practiced law for only a year, before returning to Swarthmore to teach literature and composition. In 1906, he became College librarian, a position he held through 1927, after which he served as Librarian of the Friends Historical Library.

Hayes also wrote considerable verse, much about his Chester County, Brandywine Creek, and Quaker roots. His style was straightforward, his prose sentimental yet descriptive. His writing overflows with the emotion of Place.

In 1898, Hayes published an extended poem "The Brandywine," with illustrations by Robert Shaw. Though such poetry has fallen out of fashion, "The Brandywine" has the power to evoke the romantic, even mythologized vision of nineteenth century Chester County.

In 1910, Hayes published *Brandywine Days: Or, the Shepherd's Hour-Glass,* poetry and prose recounting a summer spent on an old family farm near a tiny, decaying hamlet. This is a particularly rich resource for those who, when they travel the region's back roads, imagine days-gone-by cast in a golden glow.

A third Hayes' book, *Quaker Meeting Houses* (1909) has fifty illustrations of Quaker houses of worship, many of them Around the Delaware Arc, surviving at the turn of the century. The photographs are unified by a long poem with several sections, each section beginning "I love old Meeting-houses." The poem expresses a nostalgic sensibility from within the Quaker experience of the region's influential world-view.

These books and other works by an evocative—though forgotten—poet of the region Around the Delaware Arc can be accessed in their entirety on the World Wide Web.

"And those wide hills of storied Birmingham"

CONSERVATION AND PRESERVATION

87 - BRANDYWINE CREEK GREENWAY, CHESTER COUNTY

IN MARCH 2012, A PLAN BY the Brandywine Conservancy, on behalf of 15 Chester County municipalities and one Delaware County municipality, proposed a Brandywine Greenway. It would extend from the Delaware Arc at Chadds Ford along the general length of the Brandywine Creek and its two branches, a swath some thirty miles long and varying in width.

The plan noted: "The Brandywine Creek and surrounding landscapes function as a greenway today with thousands of acres of privately-protected open space, three major state park attractions, and over forty municipal parks and trails scattered along the corridor. The Brandywine Creek Greenway has potential to connect into a comprehensive network of greenways, open space, and trails that already exist in the state of Delaware. There, state agencies, municipalities, private corporations, and non-profit organizations have made a concerted effort to coordinate open space and recreation planning."

With lobbying taking place for a Delaware National Park in the Brandywine Valley, along a corridor extending from the Arc to Wilmington, the potential for a Greenway along the entire length of the Brandywine, anticipates an incredible landscape of protected, conserved, and planned public land, a unique in the nation and invaluable for the region Around the Delaware Arc.

The proposed Pennsylvania Greenway along the Brandywine is already extensively preserved by 90,000 acres of privately owned lands, lands held by land trusts, and lands owned by homeowners associations in Chester County. An additional 24,000 acres are in the permanent control of municipal, county, and state agencies. The Greenway would interconnect all preserved parcels.

If implemented, this plan would benefit conservation, including the quality and quantity of the entire watershed. (It supplies 140,000 people in the greater Wilmington area and in nearby Pennsylvania with water.). It would help ensure the rural quality of the landscape that already exists, including functioning farms. It would provide varied types of recreation. This is to say it would help limit development, particularly suburban sprawl.

The Brandywine Creek Greenway would further formalize and institutionalize many practices of the region, such as the interlocking easements that have kept alive foxhunting and point-to-point racing in the so-called horse country around Unionville.

88 - WOODLAWN TRUST

DELAWARE SEEKS A NATIONAL PARK, composed primarily of the Brandywine Valley of the region Around the Delaware Arc, north of Wilmington, reaching toward Chester County Pennsylvania. At the core of the proposed park is a 1,100-acre tract (880 acres in Delaware; 220 acres in Pennsylvania) established by William Poole Bancroft (1835-1928) along the Brandywine Creek north of Rockland, extending west toward Route 202 in New Castle County. Known as the Woodlawn Trust, it was sold in 2012 to the Conservation Fund with $20 million provided by the Mt. Cuba Conservancy.

Born at Rockland, William Poole Bancroft (1835-1928) made his fortune from a famous textile mill along the Brandywine in northeast Wilmington. The Woodlawn Trust he established at the beginning of the twentieth century had several philanthropic features, including the creation of modestly priced housing and gifts of Woodlawn stock to certain social organizations.

Among the provisions of the Woodlawn Trust was the fulfillment of Bancroft's personal dream "for someone to gather up the rough land along the Brandywine Creek above Rockland and hold it for the future Wilmington, a Wilmington of hundreds of thousands of people." He added, "It has been a hobby, or a concern with me, for more than twenty-six years, to endeavor to get park land for the advantage of the people of Wilmington and its vicinity."

Bancroft had urged the Du Pont Company to donate lands for public parks. When the company didn't respond, Bancroft donated 50 acres of his land to Wilmington. Bancroft advocated the city establish parks. He was instrumental in engaging celebrated landscape architect Frederick Law Olmstead to appraise sites and make recommendations.

By 1901, Bancroft had privately acquired hundreds of acres along the Brandywine, which he transferred to the Trust, now the catalyst for a National Park. In 1981, the Woodlawn Trustees transferred more than 500 acres along the Brandywine to the State of Delaware to be added to Brandywine Creek State Park.

Bancroft had grown up in a family who belonged to the Society of Friends. He continued to practice. His generous philanthropy and social vision, arguably, can be credited to integral Quaker values.

Naamans Road (Route 92) north of the Concord Pike (Route 202) in Delaware, enters the heart of the Woodlawn Trust.

89 - THE BRANDYWINE CONSERVANCY

IN THE 1960S, THE CHADDS FORD area was "threatened" with industrial development. It seemed likely that the handsome farmlands and other properties of the region Around the Delaware Arc would become prey to subdivision and development.

George Weymouth, in 1961 bought and restored an abandoned old estate (1780s) along the Big Bend of the Brandywine Creek at the Pennsylvania/Delaware Line. Toward the end of the decade, Weymouth led a campaign to secure conservation easements along his beloved Brandywine.

Known by his childhood nickname of Frolic, he was a scion of the du Pont family. His mother, Dulcinea (Deo) Ophelia Payne du Pont (1909) was one of Eugene du Pont, Jr.'s four daughters. (Weymouth's nickname Frolic relates to a family foxhound from his childhood.)

Weymouth maintains the reputation of being "the fun-loving du Pont." He is an artist of repute who paints in the realistic style of his artist friend Andrew Wyeth.

Weymouth, like many of his relatives, has a penchant for horses; his own passion involves the four in hand horse and carriage team, which he drives along the area's back roads. Because of the easements and deeds making large tracts of land accessible, this area of the Brandywine is a center of those who celebrate and drive carriages. They are known as whips or stagers.

In 1961, he inveigled two fellow bluebloods, F. I. Du Pont and William Prickett, to buy two threatened parcels of land. Weymouth then led a campaign to secure conservation easements along his stretch of the Brandywine, initiating the effort by donating his own Big Bend Property. By 1969, a five and a half mile parcel along the Brandywine was held by Brandywine Conservancy, of which Weymouth was Chairman of the Board of Trustees, a position he continues to hold.

The Conservancy next bought an old gristmill (1864) and by 1971 opened it as The Brandywine River Museum, featuring regional art, particularly of the extended Wyeth family. In recent years, the Conservancy has acquired the Kuerner Farm, Andrew Wyeth's Studio, and N.C. Wyeth's Home and Studio, which the museum includes in its programs.

The conservation easements now under the Conservancy's control total 440, protecting some 45,000 acres in Chester and Delaware counties, Pennsylvania, and in New Castle County, Delaware. In addition, the Conservancy maintains two preserves: the Waterloo Mill Preserve and the Laurels Preserve on what had once been the huge King Ranch.

The Conservancy is currently working to stitch together The Brandywine Creek Greenway, a 30-mile long green corridor extending from the Delaware state line at Chadds Ford to the state-designated Pennsylvania Highlands Mega-Greenway in the north.

The Brandywine Conservancy is an anchor for environmental protection, promotion of the regional arts, and general cultural preservation. Much of the cultural preservation suits the values of the wealthy families who own estates and large tracts of land in the Brandywine Valley.

90 - TULIP TREE WOODS

THE BRANDYWINE CREEK STATE PARK is a varied landscape—trees, rocks, and water—of 933 acres along the Brandywine Creek, three miles north of Wilmington, on property that was a turn of century du Pont (Winterthur) dairy farm.

Gifted to the State of Delaware In 1965, it contains the first two of the State's nature preserves: Freshwater Marsh and Tulip Tree Woods.

In these preserves not only are the plants and animals protected, none of the rocks and natural debris may be disturbed. However, paths easily access these two unique environments.

Tulip Tree Woods is easily accessed from the park office. After passing through a stand of a variety of trees, as well as stumps of the now decimated American Chestnut, the path enters a twenty-four acre stand of old growth tulip poplar trees. Tulip poplars are the tallest of American hardwoods.

This grove contains many old giants, a few reaching 160 feet. The short walk to this towering stand of trees renders the eye-lifting destination almost primeval.

The park office and parking is at 47 Adams Dam Rd, Wilmington, Delaware.

91 - AMERICAN SHAD

AN APT SYMBOL OF EFFORTS to conserve, preserve, and remediate the region Around the Delaware Arc is the American shad. Before the damming of Piedmont creeks, this fish was so numerous that commentators wrote of spawning runs that turned the river black. Shad provided food for the Lenni Lenape. This fish has been credited as sustaining Colonial Troops in the spring of 1778 at Valley Forge, when the shad ran up the Schuylkill River earlier than usual, leading one quip to call the shad America's "founding fish." (At the very least, the shad was to Philadelphia as the cod was to Boston.)

Shad remained relatively numerous in the Delaware River through 1901, when a long decline began. However, the Clean Water Act (1972) appears to have begun a reverse of declining shad in the Delaware River.

The shad is anadromous, spending the majority of its life in the ocean, but entering fresh water in spring to spawn. Spawning fish always return to their natal freshwater, upon sexual maturity that occurs from three to six years in saltwater. When mature, shad reach twenty to twenty four inches in length, weighing from four to eight pounds.

Females (5-6 years) lay 30,000 to 600,000 eggs into fresh water. Males (4-5 years) fertilize the eggs. Fertilized eggs drift with the current for a week or so and hatch as larvae. The larvae continue to drift with the current until maturing as juveniles. By late fall, most of the young shad had migrated to wintering areas near the ocean coast; some juvenile shad will spend a year in rivers and estuaries. After spawning, shad migrate to summer feeding grounds off the Gulf of Maine. A typical shad might travel 12,000 ocean miles during a lifetime.

Efforts to restore the spawning beds of the shad depend on completely or partially removing dams (often remnants from the eighteenth and nineteenth mills), as well as building fish ladders and rock ramps. Brandywine Creek has a targeted plan, prepared by the Brandywine Conservancy, to deal with 11 dams. If the plan were realized, shad and four other migratory fish species would return along the Brandywine and its tributaries.

Another program to restore shad spawning beds is taking place on White Clay Creek. This Creek has the distinction of being the country's first watershed (rather than river corridor) designated a Wild and Scenic River throughout its watershed.

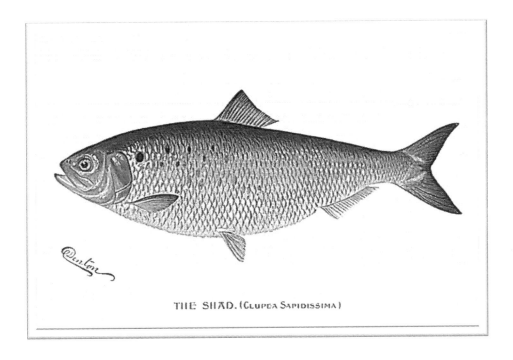

THE SHAD. (Clupea Sapidissima)

WEST OF WILMINGTON

92 - GREENBANK MILL

THE GREENBANK MILL, ALONG THE Red Clay Creek, west of Wilmington, represents the many one-owner mills that once lined the creeks of the region Around the Delaware Arc, particularly the creeks of Delaware's Mill Creek Hundred. As a working mill, Greenbank Mill had noteworthy longevity, some three hundred years of operations on the same site.

Originally, Swede's Mill, made from logs, dating from 1677, occupied the site. After the skirmish at Cooch's Bridge 1777, General Washington reputedly sent a guard to protect the Mill from the British troops advancing toward Philadelphia. In 1790, the current mill structure was erected: 50' x 39' and two and a half stories high. The original Swede's Mill remained standing adjacent to the new structure.

In 1793, the gristmill was fitted with Oliver Evans' innovative automated milling system. Evans was a local inventor whose own mill was also on Red Clay Creek. His system integrated the milling process, arguably anticipating the modern assembly line.

The owner of the Greenbank property, Robert Phillips, built a house (c. 1794), overlooking the mill. The house stands today looking much as it appeared two centuries ago.

During the anti-British, buy-American sentiment of the first two decades of the nineteenth century, leading up to the War of 1812. Phillips replaced the old mill with a new fieldstone structure to produce woolen cloth. He named his mill the Madison Factory after President Madison. The woolen business failed.

A member of the extended Phillips family bought the property. So the mill stayed in the family through 1888. In the latter years of the Phillips family operations, the site continued to mill flour, also manufacturing wooden products for carriages.

Through the mid-1960s, the owners continued to provide custom milling of grain, still using waterpower. In 1969, an arson fire ended operations.

The Greenbank Mill Associates acquired the property after the fire and set about restoring the almost destroyed Madison Factory. The project was finished in 1999. Since then, The Greenbank Mill has served as a living museum, an educational center of the integrated operations that would have taken place in the nineteenth century era of the Phillips' family. The site demonstrates the heritage of the Red Clay Creek Valley's industrial, agricultural, and social history.

The Mill also has a small herd of heritage sheep: Leicester Longwools and Delaine Merino, to keep alive the DNA of once prominent domestic animals that have nearly disappeared.

The surviving mill represents not only changing industrial strategies and manufacturing, but also the progressing technologies of milling and woodworking.

The Greenbank Mill is located at 500 Greenbank Road, Wilmington, Delaware.

93 - HALE-BURNS HOUSE

A YEAR AFTER THE CONTINENTAL Congress declared the independence of the 13 colonies, July 4, 1776, the British staged a campaign to capture Philadelphia. (The British had already captured and occupied New York City in latter half of 1776.) Under the leadership of General Sir William Howe, 15,000 troops, in August 1777 sailed from Sandy Hook, New Jersey to the northern part of the Chesapeake Bay at the mouth of the Elk River. Philadelphia lay 55 miles to the northeast.

George Washington marched an army from northern New Jersey to block the British army's advance on the seat of the Continental Congress. From Wilmington, Washington gathered reconnaissance of the British activities. After realizing that the British were not going up the Delaware River, but proceeding via the Chesapeake, he planned to intercept the British along the way.

The largest battle of the Revolutionary War (26,000 aggregate troops) was fought on September 11 near Chadds Ford, Pennsylvania— the Battle of Brandywine. After the Second Continental Congress fled to Lancaster and York, Pennsylvania, the Continental troops retreated and the British entered and occupied Philadelphia. The Second Continental Congress fled to Lancaster and then York, Pennsylvania. Washington's Continentals wintered at Valley Forge.

During Howe's march to Philadelphia, on September 3, a skirmish involving some 700 Continentals and advancing British troops under the command of General Cornwallis, occurred south of Newark, Delaware. Known as the battle of Cooch's Bridge, it was Delaware's only Revolutionary War Battle.

While the British regrouped after the skirmish, on September 6, Continental generals and officers gathered for a strategy meeting at a home on White Clay Creek, near Newark. In addition to Washington, Nathaniel Greene, Henry Knox, and the Marquis de Lafayette attended this Council of War.

The house stands behind low brick walls and along White Clay Creek. An old Sycamore to one side holds on to life despite a deeply decayed trunk. Now known as the Hale-Burns House, the 2-story brick structure along Old Stanton Road offers a reflective retreat in the midst of a developed and busy corridor between Newark and Stanton, Delaware.

The house dates from the 1750s, with a two-story addition and walk-in fireplace added two decades later. The property helps define the southern extent of the federally designated Wild and Scenic White Clay Creek.

The home is only open from noon through three o'clock, the first Wednesday of each month. However, the grounds are generally open. The address of the Hale-Byrnes House, on Old Stanton Road, is 606 Stanton-Christiana Road.

94 - DELAWARE PARK

WILLIAM DU PONT, JR. (1896-1965) WAS a leading equestrian of the region Around the Delaware Arc in the first half of the twentieth century. He bred thoroughbreds at his Bellevue Hall estate outside Wilmington. With wife Jean Liseter Austin (married 1919), du Pont developed Liseter Hall Farm in Newtown Square, Pennsylvania, which became one of the great thoroughbred stables of the 1920s and 1930s. The du Ponts raced under the name of Foxcatcher Farms. (In 2013, the long-neglected buildings of Liseter Hall Farm were razed. They had been painted matte black by the du Pont's son, John E. du Pont, who died in prison, a convicted murderer.) After their divorce in 1941, du Pont turned his attention to a massive 5,000 acre farm he created (1926) in Fair Hill, Maryland, which included a steeplechase course of du Pont's design.

Given his interests as a horseman and businessman, it is not surprising that during the Great Depression, du Pont led a group of five in advocating for a Delaware pari-mutuel racetrack.

The Delaware Racing Commission was created in 1933. Two years later, licenses could be granted for the selling of wagering pools through pari-mutuel machines. In 1936, du Pont led the group of five in the formation of Delaware Steeplechase and Race Association. They purchased a parcel of land in Stanton for the breeding and promotion of thoroughbred racehorses. The group also lobbied government officials to build a wagering racetrack on the Stanton site. Later that year, the construction of the Delaware Park Race Track began, as designed by du Pont. (He had already designed 23 racetracks.)

The tiered grandstand seated 7,500 and overlooked a one-mile dirt oval track and two grass courses. The uppermost level housed a clubhouse and turf club. Stables for more than 1,200 horses adjoined the backstretch. Delaware Park opened in 1937 with a 30-day meet and was an immediate fan favorite for its handsome grandstand and grounds, including a picnic grove.

In 1958 the grandstand seating was doubled, the clubhouse renovated, and a winner's circle added.

In more recent years, as horseracing declined, a casino was incorporated into the facility. (Delaware Park closed briefly and nearly went out of business in the 1980s.) A public golf course (2005) was sculpted along White Clay Creek's meandering route through the property.

In recent years, Delaware Park has had 81 days of nine race meetings from mid-May through late October. A special contemporary feature is the racing of Arabian horses.

Remnant charms of the original venue make Delaware Park, during the racing season, a nostalgic experience of mid-twentieth century horse racing pageantry, when the phrase "sport of kings" had a particular Delaware meaning.

Delaware Park is located at 777 Delaware Park Boulevard, Stanton.

95 - UNIVERSITY OF DELAWARE

AT THE WESTERN EDGE OF the Delaware Arc and at the bottom of the White Clay Creek State Park (3,300 acres) is Newark, Delaware, a middling sized city of some 30,000. The Delaware White Clay State Park adjoins White Clay Creek Preserve (1,255 acres) in Pennsylvania. These two parks render White Clay Creek the longest protected waterway in the country, as well as shelter for the largest remaining Piedmont forest in the region Around the Delaware Arc.

At the heart of Newark is the University of Delaware with 16,000 undergraduates and 3,500 graduate students. It is noted for its strong science, engineering, business, economics, and agriculture programs that reflect the state's history and strengths.

Its roots date back to 1743. After an 11-year hiatus, in 1870 it reemerged as a Morrill Land Grant Acts college. In 1921, under state sanction, it merged with the nearby Delaware Women's college (1913).

It has a handsome red brick, Georgian Colonial Revival campus. Of note is the unified landscaping of the campus by Marian Cruger Coffin (c. 1920), a pioneering female landscape architect. She had a strong hand in shaping The Green, a large open space running through the old campus. Newark's Main Street with restaurants and shops stroll through the campus's eastern edge. (Among her wealthy clients were several of the du Ponts, including H. Rodney Sharp. Sharp was an important benefactor for his alma mater.)

The campus has three University maintained museums.

The Old College Gallery (18 East Main Street) houses the University's main collection, including significant works by the Brandywine

School of Artists, Pre-Columbian and Southwest Native American ceramics, plus twentieth century American sculpture and ceramics.

Mechanical Hall (30 North College Avenue) houses an exciting museum, the Paul R. Jones Collection of African American Art. Of particular note are prints from the Brandywine Workshop in Philadelphia and the photographs of P. H. Polk.

The Mineralogical Museum in Penny Hall (255 Academy Street) displays some 450 specimens, emphasizing crystallized minerals and includes gems. The core, originally collected by a Tiffany executive and bought in 1919 by Irénée du Pont, Sr., was gifted to the University in 1964.

96 - MARIAN CRUGER COFFIN

MARIAN CRUGER COffiN (1876-1957) WAS A pioneering female landscape architect, who, by virtue of her connections to the du Ponts, had significant influence on the great Country Manor Estate gardens established in the region Around the Delaware Arc.

Born in Scarborough, New York, to an upper-middle class family with ties to the du Pont clan (her Mother's best friend married Henry A. du Pont), she grew up in genteel poverty. Her father squandered his income and divorced her mother. He died when she was seven. Coffin and her mother then lived at the largesse of family in Geneva, New York. The landscape and flowers of the Finger Lakes inspired her artistic sensibilities.

Weighing her prospects, she chose a career over marriage. She enrolled as a special student at the Massachusetts Institute of Technology, graduating from the architecture program at age 28. At the time, only two schools had a landscape architecture program: Harvard didn't admit women.

At MIT, Coffin was infused in the Beaux Arts aesthetic that looked to classical values as translated by the French commitment to balance and proportion, order and harmony. She also absorbed the Italian notion that the gardens and the house should be considered as a whole, complementing one another.

Even with formal training, she didn't find work with established firms when she finished the program in 1904. Using her family ties, she set out on her own.

She had a particularly strong relationship with childhood friend, Henry Francis du Pont, who in 1928 inherited the country estate of Winterthur. He had studied horticulture at

Harvard at the same time Coffin studied landscape design at MIT; they shared a love for gardens. When du Pont began (c. 1906) to manage the gardens at his family estate, he called on Coffin for counsel. One of her contributions at Winterthur is a reflective pool that was originally the family swimming pool.

Employing the notion of the gardens being an extension of the house, Coffin designed the outdoor "terrace rooms" at H. Rodney Sharp's walled estate on the northern edge of Wilmington known as Gibraltar.

Coffin also designed the Round Garden for the Lammot du Pont Copelands' country estate of Mt. Cuba.

In the region Around the Delaware Arc, Coffin's most visible legacy is the University of Delaware's Colonial Revival campus. H. Rodney Sharp had a large hand in the campus design. His friendship with Coffin recommended her to the merged College. Her plantings unified the women and men's campuses (1921). Over the years, she landscaped the extensive grounds. From 1918 through 1952, Coffin served as the University's appointed landscape architect.

97 - UDAIRY CREAMERY

A VISIT TO THE UNIVERSITY of Delaware campus, the city of Newark, or the White Clay Creek attractions might also include a visit to the UDairy Creamery.

Since 2008, the UDairy Creamery has been churning its own ice cream made from the milk of its own cows, as part of the University's College of Agriculture and Natural Resources program.

The milk is shipped to Cumberland Dairy in Cumberland, New Jersey, where it is pasteurized, homogenized, and transformed into a thickened ice cream base. Returned to the University Creamery, it is made into ice cream. The freshly churned ice cream is sold by the scoop and container at a new UDairy Creamery (2011). The Creamery's motto is "from the cow to the cone."

There are regularly available flavors: vanilla, chocolate, strawberry, black raspberry, butter pecan, mint chocolate chip, peach, and coffee. There is a changing array of specialty flavors with enticing combinations of ingredients, such as "The First State Cobbler" that includes peach ice cream with blueberry swirl and cinnamon crumb topping.

The UDairy Creamery store is located on the South Campus near the sports facilities at 535 South College Avenue and open year round. Eat indoors, outside on picnic tables, or perhaps at a bench in the adjacent Botanic Gardens. The store sells coffee drinks. It is also the sole outlet for products made from the University's sheep and bees.

There is no better ice cream in the region Around the Delaware Arc.

THREE REGIONAL FOODS

98 - SUBMARINE AND STEAK SANDWICHES

WHILE VISITING THE REGION AROUND the Delaware Arc, to eat like a local, a submarine or steak sandwich is *de rigueur*. One of the shops that provides an authentic and full experience is the Claymont Steak Shop (since 1966) just south of the Raskob House (The Patio), now Archmere Academy.

The décor is not fancy, though it is spacious and clean. To one side, an open area permits the visitor to witness the cooking and assembling of these famous sandwiches, along with other Italian-themed and regional foods.

The eponymous star of the shop is the Claymont Cheese Steak, thinly sliced rib eye steak fried on a grill and served on an Italian roll. It is piled with fried or raw onions, ketchup, pickles, lettuce, tomatoes, hot peppers, sweet peppers, or mayonnaise. The diner's choice of any of the sandwich's ingredients is made at the counter, where the order is placed and paid for.

There are other steak sandwiches choices: chicken cheese steak, buffalo chicken cheese steak, pizza cheese steak, mushroom cheese steak, and pepper and cheese steak.

Subs (as the locals call the submarine sandwich) cannot get any fresher. The shop uses high quality, sliced-to-order meats and cheeses. They are served in baked Italian rolls and topped with lettuce, tomato, onion, pickles, sweet peppers, hot peppers, oregano, oil or mayonnaise. The choices include ham and cheese, regular (cooked salami, cooked ham, and American cheese), special (capicola, Genoa salami, cooked ham and provolone cheese), cheese (provolone or mixed), turkey, roast beef, veggie, and tuna.

While the subs and steak sandwiches are the shop's primary foods, there are a host of other possibilities, including soup, pasta, dinner platters, appetizers, salads, wings, and hot grinder sandwiches.

There is a small controversy regarding the name of the region's oversized sandwiches. Delawareans use *submarine*, as in the case of the Claymont Steak Shop. Pennsylvanians, however, favor *hoagie*, tracing the origins of the sandwich to Philadelphia's Hog Island shipyard, circa World War I.

The original Claymont location is 3526 Philadelphia Pike, Claymont, Delaware. A second location is 57 Elkton Road, Newark, Delaware, near the University of Delaware.

99 – SCRAPPLE

Of the various regional foods Around the Delaware Arc, scrapple ranks as among the most indigenous. Scrapple combines cornmeal with pork offal and scraps, congealed into slabs that are sliced and fried.

Scrapple developed in the seventeenth and eighteenth centuries among Germans living in the farm regions outside of Philadelphia, notably Chester County. Recipes vary, but the original process is at the core: the boiling of offal (particularly liver) and trimmings; dicing the cooked meats; boiling the corn meal in the reserved broth; combining the diced meat and cooked meal into loaves with seasonings (notably sage, thyme, and savory); and cooling the mixture until it congeals.

Scrapple is frequently a breakfast side, but is also incorporated into sandwiches.

Scrapple represents the rural roots of the region Around the Delaware Arc: farming traditions, frugality, and a German influence that have been part of the region since the earliest years of Penn's grant.

The region has a familiar phrase, when asked, of what scrapple is made of: "Everything but the oink." And then a litany begins: "Snouts, Tails, Hearts, Lips, Ears, Eyeballs, Livers, Spleens, Tongues…."

Diners are a good place to find breakfast scrapple. Some prefer to douse their scrapple in syrup.

100 - IRISH POTATO CANDY

DISTINCTIVE FOODS OF THE REGION Around the Delaware Arc remember various immigrant groups. German settlers developed scrapple. Italians perfected the submarine and steak sandwiches. Irish settlers have a curious confection known as Irish potato candy.

The origin of this seasonal treat looks to Philadelphia more than a century ago and the commemoration of the Irish Potato Famine (1845-1851) that drove many Irish to emigrate to other countries. Philadelphia had a large Irish community already and was a primary port of entry for many Irish who came to America. These mostly Catholic immigrants added fuel to the Nativism that reached a crescendo in a famous riot of 1844, just a year before the Potato Famine further swelled Philadelphia's Irish population.

Irish potato candy resembles a miniature potato. It has several variations, but the now familiar version has a coconut cream center and may also include nuts. Shaped into a small potato, it is rolled in cinnamon, making a remarkable facsimile of its namesake.

A family candy shop, Christopher Chocolates (3519 West Chester Pike, Newtown Square) that opened in 1986, at the request of customers, began hand production of this bite size candy. The demand boomed and the family began to produce in commercial quantities under the name of Oh Ryans. Their factory is now located in Linwood. The Newtown Square store always has a supply on hand for the confectionary curious.

Boxes of the Irish Potato candy appear in grocery stores and other shops in the region Around the Delaware Arc in anticipation of St. Patrick's Day. Each year the company makes some 80,000 pounds of this unique product at a Linwood, Delaware County factory.

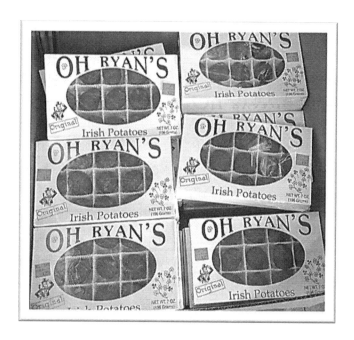

The Good Life

101 - *The Good Life*

The region Around the Delaware Arc has inspired varied visions of the Good Life.

William Penn, even before his 1682 arrival, thoughtfully planned Philadelphia with spacious lots of an acre or half acre. He devised a starter house that acquired the name of Penn Plan House. Penn arranged streets in an orderly grid pattern with four sections around a center square. Each section had its own square (or public land). He imagined a country town, such as he had experienced in Ireland, when his family had been exiled from England by Cromwell.

Penn also called his land grant colony a "Holy Experiment" founded on principles of The Religious Society of Friends (Quakers) that included honorable treatment of the indigenous people who inhabited Pennsylvania before Penn arrived and a tolerant acceptance of other Christian sects.

A Quaker government endured in Pennsylvania through 1756, and significant Quaker values infused the region through the nineteenth century.

Penn's Holy Experiment was mythologized by the Quaker Artist Edward Hicks (1780-1849) who joined Penn's notion of a Holy Experiment to words from the book of Isaiah, maintaining that someday the child will lie down with the lion and the lamb. This prophetic vision, known as the Peaceable Kingdom, resulted in more than 60 renderings by Hicks in the early decades of the nineteenth century. Some of the Peaceable Kingdom paintings portrayed Penn and a Lenni Lenape chief signing "the Great Treaty" in the background.

When the du Pont family fled America for the United States arriving on January 1, 1800, the *pater noster* of the family, Pierre Samuel had the plan of establishing an ideal French émigré community to be called *Pontania*. Instead, his son E.I. established a black powder company and family dynasty in Wilmington, Delaware. Tightly knit by intermarriage and fabulous riches, the du Pont family realized their own version of the good life, building grand country manors throughout the Brandywine Valley in the early decades of the twentieth century.

At the turn of the century, while the du Ponts were transforming their interest from explosives to chemicals, there was a reaction to industrialization that coalesced in an Arts and Crafts (American Craftsman) movement, as well as economic experimentation based on the Single Tax theories of Philadelphian Henry George. The sculptor Frank Stephens and the architect Will Price, with the financial assistance from the soap magnate Joseph Fels, founded the single-tax community of Arden, Delaware. Under Stephens's leadership, Arden welcomed a diversity of progressives and radicals. Arden attracted Scott Nearing as an early resident. Nearing became the father of the Back to the Land movement of the second half of the twentieth century. His signature phrase became "the good life." He remembered Arden as "the good life in miniature."

Will Price moved on to found the Arts and Crafts Movement community of Rose Valley, Pennsylvania, that included an example of the "Democrat House," his version of an ideal middle class home suited to the nuclear family (without servants) that was defining American culture at the turn of the century. Price's Rose Valley was a well-conceived community that emulated William Morris's influential design ideas, including guilds of artisans. A few artisans worked at Rose Valley, but it failed to attract a continuing contingent.

A working class vision of the good life continues to be realized in Marcus Hook, Pennsylvania's Viscose Village, built by the pioneering synthetic fiber company, American Viscose. Something of a company town and something of a Garden City, Viscose Village was modeled on British precedents and has an English Domestic Revival overall style.

Though the plant across the street closed in 1970, Viscose Village has retained a distinct and strong sense of community.

The Wyeth family of Chadds Ford, Pennsylvania realized an artistic version of the good life. Howard Pyle's summer school helped establish the notion of a Brandywine School of Illustration led by Pyle. Beginning in 1908 on 18 acres, N.C. Wyeth, a Pyle student, headed three generations of Wyeths and in-laws, including son Andrew, who achieved fame for his iconic paintings, many depicting a small piece, mood, or moment of the Brandywine countryside.

Circumstance and landscape have made the region Around the Delaware Arc an apt medium for varied visions of the Good Life.

AUTHOR'S POSTSCRIPT

THE PLACE WHERE I STARTED

I WAS BORN IN THE Crozer Hospital in Chester, Pennsylvania, and for two years lived in Boothwyn, Delaware County, Pennsylvania. My father worked in the nearby Sun Oil Marcus Hook refinery. From age two until I was twenty-one, I lived on the Delaware side of the fabled Arc. The schools I attended were in the Alfred I. Du Pont Special School District. My junior high chemistry class was included in a Du Pont Company ("Better Things for Better Living through Chemistry") television commercial in the early 1960s. I played youth baseball in Claymont. When first married, my wife Ellie and I lived in a picturesque cottage in Arden. I took my undergraduate degree from the University of Delaware at Newark. This region is my natal home, where I lived the first twenty-one years of my life Around the Delaware Arc.

Now, at the age of sixty-five, I've retired. With Ellie, I've returned to a small bungalow on Foulk Road at the northern reach of Wilmington, Delaware, to care for my ninety-six and ninety-seven year old parents. We live together in the 1950 home my father built largely by hand. When I grew up there, the northern boundary of my parents' 7/8th acre property was literally a small segment of the Delaware Arc.

My return after a forty-five year sojourn provides me with an apt opportunity to consider what I've done with my life and career, as well as reflect on the influences of the first third of my life that bent me in certain ways.

T. S. Eliot's familiar words summarize the process of reflection and reengagement that confronts me on my return:

> *We shall not cease from exploration*
> *And the end of all our exploring*
> *Will be to arrive where we started*
> *And know the place for the first time.*

For me now, Eliot's words apply to Self and Place—the intertwining and mutuality of both, how a region around the Delaware Arc is rich in emotional meaning, as well as continuing influence.

TOPOPHILIA

FOR THIRTY-FIVE YEARS I was an active Unitarian minister. I spent five and a half years in Youngstown, Ohio, a crumbling, former steel town in Eastern Ohio and thirty years in Hinsdale, Illinois, a prosperous suburb 15 miles west of Chicago. At the beginning of my career, I identified as a Religious Humanist; at the end, I called myself a practitioner of Natural Religion true to Nature and Human Nature. A favorite theme of the Natural Religion that I spoke about in Youngstown and Hinsdale was Space and Place. In the late 1990s, I wrote a book, *A Place of Your Own*—a how-to resource for creating Sacred Space in one's own home.

Over three decades, I increasingly appreciated the historical and architectural significance of my Hinsdale Church-Home, with the House Beautiful aesthetic it embodies plus the turn of the century Arts and Crafts aesthetic in which it is ensconced. I also came to see the Chicago region as the *axis mundi* of North America's Natural History, earning that Heartland city the moniker of Nature's Metropolis.

At first, in musing about sacred Space and Place, I intuitively spoke of spiritual significance. I subsequently learned there is a subset of the academic discipline of Geography that draws on other disciplines, including philosophy, art, psychology, and religion in relation to study Space and Place.

The resulting Humanist Geography is a relatively new (1970) branch of geography that concerns itself with interrelations between Nature/Place and Human Beings. From this eclectic approach, Places through which people move define a Space. It seems self-evident now but Humanist Geography only recently established that Places need a Space to exist, while Space is defined by the Places it contains.

Human beings have an emotional response to Places (*fields of care*) and fill a Space with multiple meanings, though those meanings may be intangible rather than palpable. An early and influential proponent of Humanist Geography, Yi-Fu Tuan, in the 1970s promoted the word *topophilia*, meaning "emotional connections between physical environment and human beings" to launch Humanist Geography. In this regard, Places may be referred to as "territories of meaning" that result in affection and attraction.

Topophilia resonates to an ancient term *genius loci* that in Latin means "spirit of place." For the Roman's classical imagination, the world was Sacred Space. In this Sacred Space, a pantheon of deities resided in many particular Places. Every Place—river, glen, grove of trees, mountain plus village or town—had an associated sacred/divine presence that offered protection and gave identity, rendering a Place distinctive and numinous.

The Romans were not unique in associating resident spirits to particular locations. That many cultures also did so suggests a phenomenon of the human condition to have emotional responses to Place that includes a quest for and discovery of natural meaning.

For the ancients, a *genius loci*, expressed via mythology what Humanist Geography now analyzes subjectively.

Before I could write a reflective essay about the influence that the place of the first 20 years of my life exerted on me, I realized I needed to explore anew the region Around the Delaware Arc, with seeing eyes enhanced by years of experience and knowledge.

Ellie and I set out on an adventure of renewal and discovery. In this book, I have chronicled that exploration. As a result, my love for the region Around the Delaware Arc has expanded. I hope this collection will help you better realize a love for the many unique places that converge and intertwine AROUND THE DELAWARE ARC.

Made in the USA
Lexington, KY
02 October 2013